श्रीमद्भगवद्गीता

षोडशोऽध्यायः – दैवासुरसम्पद्विभागयोगः

śrīmadbhagavadgītā

ṣoḍaśo'dhyāyaḥ - daivāsurasampadvibhāgayogaḥ

Bhagavad-Gītā Chapter Sixteen

Sanskrit Text with Transliteration, Translation & Brief Commentary

गीता-मूलम् १६

Gītā-Mūlam 16

गीता या मधुसूदनप्रभविणी युक्ता परं ब्रह्मणि
gītā yā madhusūdana-prabhaviṇī yuktā paraṁ brahmaṇi
या कृष्णेन कृताऽखिलं नयनवद् वक्षोऽतिगूढार्थिनी ।
yā kṛṣṇena kṛtā-'khilaṃ nayanavad vakṣo-'tigūḍhārthinī ,
या लोकत्रयस्य मार्गविधिनी धर्मस्य साक्षात्पथा
yā lokatrayasya marga-vidhinī dharmasya sākṣāt-pathā ,
सा श्रीकृष्णमुखारविन्दजनिता तस्याः मूलं प्रयच्छामि ॥
sā śrī-kṛṣṇa-mukhāravinda-janitā tasyāḥ mūlaṁ prayacchāmi .

That Gītā—which's born from Madhusūdana -- who exists in Oneness with Braham;
that Gītā—which's uttered by Krishna -- of profound visions of deep mysteries concealed within;
that Gītā—which lights the Dharma-path across the threefold world;
that Gītā—that sprung from Shri Krishna's lotus-lips
—to Her sacred roots I proceed and take refuge.

Belongs to ______________________

॥ यतो धर्मस्ततो जयः - एकं-सनातन-धर्म विजयः ॥
- yato dharmastato jayaḥ -- ekaṁ sanātana-dharma vijayaḥ -
- Where Dharma abides Victory abides -- Victory unto Ekam-Sanātana-Dharma -

Published by: only **RAMA** only

Title: **Gita-Mulam 16 – Bhagavad Gita Chapter Sixteen**
Sub-Title: **Sanskrit Text with Transliteration, Translation & Brief Commentary**
A No-Opinions Commentary. Only Facts. Bhagavad-Gita As It Truly Is.
An Excellent Resource for Sectless Gita-Study (With Wide Margin for Taking Notes)

गीता-मूलम् १६
gītā-mūlam 16
श्रीमद्भगवद्गीता षोडशोऽध्यायः – दैवासुरसम्पद्विभागयोगः
śrīmadbhagavadgītā ṣoḍaśo'dhyāyaḥ – daivāsurasampadvibhāgayogaḥ

Authors: Adarsh Saxena & Vijay Kumar

Identifiers

ISBN: 978-1-945739-76-7 (Paperback)

—o—

Books in the Gita-Mulam series: Gita-Mulam **01** (isbn: **979-8-90060-741-2**). Gita-Mulam **02** (isbn: **979-8-90060-742-9**). Gita-Mulam **03** (isbn: **979-8-90060-743-6**). Gita-Mulam **04** (isbn: **979-8-90060-744-3**). Gita-Mulam **05** (isbn: **978-1-945739-75-0**). Gita-Mulam **06** (isbn: **979-8-90060-746-7**). Gita-Mulam **07** (isbn: **979-8-90060-747-4**). Gita-Mulam **08** (isbn: **979-8-90060-748-1**). Gita-Mulam **09** (isbn: **979-8-90060-749-8**). Gita-Mulam **10** (isbn: **979-8-90060-750-4**). Gita-Mulam **11** (isbn: **979-8-90060-751-1**). Gita-Mulam **12** (isbn: **978-1-945739-52-1**). Gita-Mulam **13** (isbn: **979-8-90060-753-5**). Gita-Mulam **14** (isbn: **979-8-90060-754-2**). Gita-Mulam **15** (isbn: **978-1-945739-51-4**). Gita-Mulam **16** (isbn: **978-1-945739-76-7**). Gita-Mulam **17** (isbn: **979-8-90060-757-3**). Gita-Mulam **18** (isbn: **979-8-90060-758-0**). All 18 books will be released by Fall 2026. Some books might become available sooner, please check your bookstore/online.

—o—

Our Bhagavad-Gitā Books:
Bhagavad Gita, The Holy Book of Hindus, with Sanskrit Text, English Translation & Transliteration, No Commentary.
- **ISBN: 978-1-945739-36-1 / 978-1-945739-37-8** (Paperback/Hardback. Book Size 6.14"x9.21"x190 pages)
- **ISBN: 978-1-945739-39-2** (For Gitā Journaling. 8"x8"x390 pages)
- **ISBN: 978-1-945739-43-9** (Convenient Pocket-Sized Edition. 4"x6"x180 pages)
- **ISBN: 978-1-945739-40-8** (Legacy Book. 7.5"x9.25"x246 pages)
- **ISBN: 978-1-945739-55-2 / 978-1-945739-56-9** (Paperback/Hardback. For Note-Taking. 7.5"x9.25"x190 pages)

Also Available:
- **Tulsi Ramayana—Hindu Holy Book:** Ramcharitmanas with English Translation (ISBNs: 978-1-945739-**60-6**, 978-1-945739-**61-3**)
- **Ramcharitmanas - Large/Medium/Small** (No Translation)
- **Sundarakanda:** The Fifth-Ascent of Tulsi Ramayana (ISBNs: 978-1-945739-**05-7**, 978-1-945739-**15-6**)
- **Rama Hymns:** Hanuman-Chalisa, Rāma-Raksha-Stotra, etc. (ISBNs: 978-1-945739-**25-5**, 978-1-945739-**09-5**)
- **Vivekachudamani, Fiery Crest-Jewel of Wisdom** (ISBNs: 978-1-945739-**44-6**, 978-1-945739-**45-3**, 978-1-945739-**41-5**)
- **Ashtavakra Gītā, the Fiery Octave** (ISBNs: 978-1-945739-**46-0**, 978-1-945739-**47-7**, 978-1-945739-**42-2**)
- **Legacy Books - Endowment of Devotion (several):** Journal Books of sacred Hindu Hymns around which the Holy-Name Rama Name can be written; available in Paperback and Hardcover for: **Hanuman Chalisa** (ISBN: 1945739274/ 1945739940) **Sundara-Kanda** (ISBN: 1945739908/ 1945739916) **Rama-Raksha-Stotra** (ISBN: 1945739991/ 1945739967) **Bhushundi-Ramayana** (ISBN: 1945739983/ 1945739975) **Nama-Ramayanam** (ISBN: 1945739304/ 1945739959)
- **Rama Jayam - Likhita Japam Rama-Nama Mala alongside Sacred Hindu Texts (several):** Books for writing the 'Rama' Name 100,000 Times. Rama Jayam - Likhita Japam:Rama-Nama Mala. Available in Book Size 8"x10" (Paperback) for: **Hanuman Chalisa** (ISBN: 1945739169) **Rama Raksha Stotra** (ISBN: 1945739185) **Nama-Ramayanam** (ISBN: 1945739045) **Ramashtakam** (ISBN: 1945739177) **Rama Shatanama Stotra** (ISBN: 1945739266) **Rama-Shatnamavalih** (ISBN: 1945739134) **Simple (I)** (ISBN: 1945739142)
- **Likhita Japam** - Paperback books for writing the 'Rama' Name in dotted grids: **One-Lettered Rama Mantra**, Book Size 8"x10" (ISBN: 1945739312) **Two-Lettered Rama Mantra,** Book Size 8"x10" (ISBN: 1945739320) **Three-Lettered Rama Mantra,** Book Size 8"x10" (ISBN: 1945739339) **Four-Lettered Rama Mantra,** Book Size 8"x10" (ISBN: 1945739347) **Simple (II)** Book Size 7.5"x9.25" (ISBN: 1945739193) **Simple (III)** Book Size 8"x8" (ISBN: 1945739282) **Simple (IV)** Book Size 8.5"x8.5" (ISBN: 1945739878) **Simple (V)** Book Size 8.5"x11" (ISBN: 1945739924)

CONTENTS

गीता-मूलम् १६
gītā-mūlam 16
श्रीमद्भगवद्गीता षोडशोऽध्यायः – दैवासुरसम्पद्विभागयोगः
śrīmadbhagavadgītā ṣoḍaśo'dhyāyaḥ - daivāsurasampadvibhāgayogaḥ

bhagavad-gītā

श्रीमद्भगवद्गीता

प्रथमोऽध्यायः - अर्जुनविषादयोगः

धृतराष्ट्र उवाच –

धर्मक्षेत्रे कुरुक्षेत्रे समवेता युयुत्सवः ।
मामकाः पाण्डवाश्चैव किमकुर्वत सञ्जय ॥ १-१ ॥

सञ्जय उवाच –

दृष्ट्वा तु पाण्डवानीकं व्यूढं दुर्योधनस्तदा ।
आचार्यमुपसङ्गम्य राजा वचनमब्रवीत् ॥ १-२ ॥
पश्यैतां पाण्डुपुत्राणामाचार्य महतीं चमूम् ।
व्यूढां द्रुपदपुत्रेण तव शिष्येण धीमता ॥ १-३ ॥
अत्र शूरा महेष्वासा भीमार्जुनसमा युधि ।
युयुधानो विराटश्च द्रुपदश्च महारथः ॥ १-४ ॥
धृष्टकेतुश्चेकितानः काशिराजश्च वीर्यवान् ।
पुरुजित्कुन्तिभोजश्च शैब्यश्च नरपुङ्गवः ॥ १-५ ॥
युधामन्युश्च विक्रान्त उत्तमौजाश्च वीर्यवान् ।
सौभद्रो द्रौपदेयाश्च सर्व एव महारथाः ॥ १-६ ॥
अस्माकं तु विशिष्टा ये तान्निबोध द्विजोत्तम ।
नायका मम सैन्यस्य संज्ञार्थं तान्ब्रवीमि ते ॥ १-७ ॥
भवान्भीष्मश्च कर्णश्च कृपश्च समितिञ्जयः ।
अश्वत्थामा विकर्णश्च सौमदत्तिस्तथैव च ॥ १-८ ॥
अन्ये च बहवः शूरा मदर्थे त्यक्तजीविताः ।
नानाशस्त्रप्रहरणाः सर्वे युद्धविशारदाः ॥ १-९ ॥
अपर्याप्तं तदस्माकं बलं भीष्माभिरक्षितम् ।
पर्याप्तं त्विदमेतेषां बलं भीमाभिरक्षितम् ॥ १-१० ॥

द्वितीयोऽध्यायः - साङ्ख्ययोगः

तृतीयोऽध्यायः - कर्मयोगः

चतुर्थोऽध्यायः - ज्ञानकर्मसंन्यासयोगः

पञ्चमोऽध्यायः - संन्यासयोगः

षष्ठोऽध्यायः - ध्यानयोगः

सप्तमोऽध्यायः - ज्ञानविज्ञानयोगः

अष्टमोऽध्यायः - अक्षरब्रह्मयोगः

नवमोऽध्यायः - राजविद्याराजगुह्ययोगः

दशमोऽध्यायः - विभूतियोगः

एकादशोऽध्यायः - विश्वरूपदर्शनयोगः

द्वादशोऽध्यायः - भक्तियोगः

त्रयोदशोऽध्यायः - क्षेत्रक्षेत्रज्ञविभागयोगः

चतुर्दशोऽध्यायः - गुणत्रयविभागयोगः

पञ्चदशोऽध्यायः - पुरुषोत्तमयोगः

षोडशोऽध्यायः - दैवासुरसम्पद्विभागयोगः

सप्तदशोऽध्यायः - श्रद्धात्रयविभागयोगः

अष्टादशोऽध्यायः - मोक्षसंन्यासयोगः

ॐ ॐ ॐ ॐ ॐ ॐ ॐ ॐ ॐ ॐ ॐ ॐ ॐ ॐ ॐ ॐ ॐ ॐ

—ॐ— ध्यानम् —ॐ— dhyānam —ॐ—

—ॐ—ॐ—ॐ—ॐ—ॐ—ॐ—

ॐ INVOCATIONS

ॐ श्री परमात्मने नमः
— om śrī paramātmane namaḥ —
[Om—I bow down to the Supreme-Energy, Supreme-Being]

त्वमेव माता च पिता त्वमेव । त्वमेव बंधुश्च सखा त्वमेव ।
tvameva mātā ca pitā tvameva , tvameva baṁdhuśca sakhā tvameva ,
त्वमेव विद्या द्रविणं त्वमेव । त्वमेव सर्वं मम देवदेव ॥
tvameva vidyā draviṇaṁ tvameva , tvameva sarvaṁ mama devadeva .

Thou art my mother and my father, Thou alone my kin, kith, friend; Thou alone my wisdom, knowledge, wealth; Thou alone—O God of gods—my all, and everything!

—ॐ—

शान्ताकारं भुजगशयनं पद्मनाभं सुरेशं । विश्वाधारं गगनसदृशं मेघवर्णं शुभाङ्गम् ।
śāntākāraṁ bhujagaśayanaṁ padmanābhaṁ sureśaṁ
viśvādhāraṁ gaganasadṛśaṁ meghavarṇaṁ śubhāṅgam ,
लक्ष्मीकान्तं कमलनयनं योगिभिर्ध्यानगम्यं । वन्दे विष्णुं भवभयहरं सर्वलोकैकनाथम् ॥
lakṣmīkāntaṁ kamalanayanaṁ yogibhirdhyānagamyaṁ
vande viṣṇuṁ bhavabhayaharaṁ sarvalokaikanātham .

I venerate Shri Vishnu—of a serene appearance who slumbers upon the serpent *Shesha-Nāga*, from whose navel has sprung the lotus of creation, who presides over as the God of gods, who is the substratum of the universe, boundless and infinite like the sky. Of a dark hue like the clouds, of a form radiating everlasting auspiciousness, with eyes beautiful like lotus petals, who is the beloved of Devī Lakshmī, who is reachable only through devotional meditation by Yogīs, who removes all fears of worldly existence—upon Him, Vishnu, the One Great Lord of all the worlds, I meditate.

—ॐ—

यं ब्रह्मा वरुणेन्द्ररुद्रमरुतः स्तुन्वन्ति दिव्यैः स्तवैः
yaṁ brahmā varuṇendrarudramarutaḥ stunvanti divyaiḥ stavaiḥ
वेदैः साङ्गपदक्रमोपनिषदैर्गायन्ति यं सामगाः ।
vedaiḥ sāṅgapadakramopaniṣadairgāyanti yaṁ sāmagāḥ ,
ध्यानावस्थिततद्गतेन मनसा पश्यन्ति यं योगिनो
dhyānāvasthitatadgatena manasā paśyanti yaṁ yogino
यस्यान्तं न विदुः सुरासुरगणा देवाय तस्मै नमः ॥
yasyāntaṁ na viduḥ surāsuragaṇā devāya tasmai namaḥ .

Unto That Supreme—whom Brahammā, Varuna, Indra, Rudra and the Mārutas praise with excellent holy hymns; who is versified throughout the Vedas and Upanishads by the chanters of Sāma; who—in perfect meditations deep—the

yogis see within their own minds while absorbed in "That-One"; whose beginning and end, even gods and demi-gods never know of—unto That Supreme-Being, I offer my many venerations.

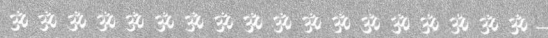

—ॐ— स्तुतिः —ॐ— stutiḥ —ॐ—

—ॐ—ॐ—ॐ—ॐ—ॐ—ॐ—

VENERATIONS

—ॐ—

पार्थाय प्रतिबोधितां भगवता नारायणेन स्वयम्
pārthāya pratibodhitāṁ bhagavatā nārāyaṇena svayam
व्यासेनग्रथितां पुराणमुनिना मध्ये महाभारते ।
vyāsenagrathitāṁ purāṇamuninā madhye mahābhārate ,
अद्वैतामृतवर्षिणीं भगवतीमष्टादशाध्यायिनीम्
advaitāmṛtavarṣiṇīṁ bhagavatīmaṣṭādaśādhyāyinīm
अम्ब त्वामनुसन्दधामि भगवद्गीते भवेद्वेषिणीम् ॥
amba tvāmanusandadhāmi bhagavadgīte bhavedveṣiṇīm .

O Thou Bhagavad-Gītā—with whom Pārtha was enlightened by the Lord Nārāyana himself; who was integrated into the Mahābhārata by the ancient sage Vyāsa; O Thou blessed Mother—who with her eighteen Cantos shower humanity with the nectar of Advaita; O Thou destroyer of rebirths, upon Thee—O Bhagavad-Gītā, O loving Mother—I meditate.

—ॐ—

नमोऽस्तु ते व्यास विशालबुद्धे फुल्लारविन्दायतपत्रनेत्र ।
namo'stu te vyāsa viśālabuddhe phullāravindāyatapatranetra ,
येन त्वया भारततैलपूर्णः प्रज्वालितो ज्ञानमयः प्रदीपः ॥
yena tvayā bhāratatailapūrṇaḥ prajvālito jñānamayaḥ pradīpaḥ .

Salutations to Thee O Vyāsa—of a mighty intellect and with eyes large like the petals of a full-blossomed lotus; by whom has been forever lit in this world the Lamp-of-Wisdom, filled with the oil in the form of the great epic: Mahābhārata.

— ॐ —

प्रपन्नपारिजाताय तोत्रवेत्रैकपाणये ।
prapannapārijātāya totravetraikapāṇaye ,
ज्ञानमुद्राय कृष्णाय गीतामृतदुहे नमः ॥
jñānamudrāya kṛṣṇāya gītāmṛtaduhe namaḥ .

He—who is the wish-granting tree of the suppliant—in whose one hand is held the rope for cow and with the other hand who holds the Yogic posture of *Jnana*—who is the milcher of the nectar known as Gītā—unto Him, Krishna, my repeated venerations.

— ॐ —

सर्वोपनिषदो गावो दोग्धा गोपालनन्दनः ।
sarvopaniṣado gāvo dogdhā gopālanandanaḥ ,
पार्थो वत्सः सुधीर्भोक्ता दुग्धं गीतामृतं महत् ॥
pārtho vatsaḥ sudhīrbhoktā dugdhaṁ gītāmṛtaṁ mahat .

All the Upanishads are the cows; the milcher is the joy of cowherds, Krishna; Pārtha is the calf; the man of purified understanding is the partaker; and the milk is verily the supreme nectar known as Gītā.

— ॐ —

वसुदेवसुतं देवं कंसचाणूरमर्दनम् ।
vasudevasutaṁ devaṁ kaṁsacāṇūramardanam ,
देवकीपरमानन्दं कृष्णं वन्दे जगद्गुरुम् ॥
devakīparamānandaṁ kṛṣṇaṁ vande jagadgurum .

I worship the charioteer, the Lord-God, the destroyer of Kamsa and Chānura, the supreme joy of Devakī, the son of Vāsudeva—Shri Krishna, the Universal Guru.

— ॐ —

भीष्मद्रोणतटा जयद्रथजला गान्धारनीलोत्पला
bhīṣmadroṇataṭā jayadrathajalā gāndhāranīlotpalā
शल्यग्राहवती कृपेण वहनी कर्णेन वेलाकुला ।
śalyagrāhavatī kṛpeṇa vahanī karṇena velākulā ,
अश्वत्थामविकर्णघोरमकरा दुर्योधनावर्तिनी
aśvatthāmavikarṇaghoramakarā duryodhanāvartinī
सोत्तीर्णा खलु पाण्डवैरणनदी कैवर्तकः केशवः ॥
sottīrṇā khalu pāṇḍavairaṇanadī kaivartakaḥ keśavaḥ .

That terrible battle-river—which had Bhīṣma and Droṇa as its two banks, and Jayadrathaja as its waters; which had the king of Gāndhāra as its blue lotus, and Śalya as its shark; whose currents and billows were Kṛipā and Karṇa; which had Aśvatthāmā and Vikarṇa as its terrible alligators; and of which Duryodhana was the deadly whirlpool—that ferocious river could be forded by the Pāṇḍavas only because they had Keśava as their helmsman.

— ॐ —

पाराशर्यवचः सरोजममलं गीतार्थगन्धोत्कटं
pārāśaryavacaḥ sarojamamalaṁ gītārthagandhotkaṭaṁ
नानाख्यानककेसरं हरिकथासम्बोधनाबोधितम्।
nānākhyānakakesaraṁ harikathāsambodhanābodhitam ।
लोके सज्जनषट्पदैरहरहः पेपीयमानं मुदा
loke sajjanaṣaṭpadairaharahaḥ pepīyamānaṁ mudā
भूयाद्भारतपङ्कजं कलिमलप्रध्वंसिनः श्रेयसे ॥
bhūyādbhāratapaṅkajaṁ kalimalapradhvaṁsinaḥ śreyase .

May this Lotus called Mahābhārata—which was born on the lake of the words of Vyāsa—which is perfumed with the fragrance of the Purport-of-Gītā—which has its innumerous stories as the pollen—which became fully bloomed through the discourses of Hari—which is the destroyer of the sins of the Kali-Yuga—which is everyday partaken joyously by the bees in the shape of good people of the world—may it bestow all goodness upon us.

— ॐ —

मूकं करोति वाचालं पङ्गुं लङ्घयते गिरिम् ।
mūkaṁ karoti vācālaṁ paṅguṁ laṅghayate girim ,
यत्कृपा तमहं वन्दे परमानन्दमाधवम् ॥
yatkṛpā tamahaṁ vande paramānandamādhavam .

I salute the Supreme-Being of the nature of supreme bliss, by whose very grace the dumb become eloquent and the cripples step across mountains.

— ॐ —

ॐ पूर्णमदः पूर्णमिदं पूर्णात् पूर्णमुदच्यते ।
om pūrṇamadaḥ pūrṇamidaṁ pūrṇāt pūrṇamudacyate ,
पूर्णस्य पूर्णमादाय पूर्णमेवावशिष्यते ।
pūrṇasya pūrṇamādāya pūrṇamevāvaśiṣyate ,
ॐ शान्तिः शान्तिः शान्तिः ॥
om śāntiḥ śāntiḥ śāntiḥ .

Om—That One (the unmanifest Brahma)—is infinite, complete, Entire; this (the manifest universe) is entire; And from That One fullness has emerged this entire universe here; And even when this entirety here is taken out of that One-Entire, It still abides complete in all Its entireness! Om, peace—let there be tranquility all around me!

— ॐ — ॐ — ॐ — ॐ — ॐ — ॐ — ॐ — ॐ — ॐ —

ॐ The Gītā Journey Thus Far

— ॐ तत सत ॐ —

Amidst the vast ocean of sacred knowledge bestowed by the seers of Sanātana-Dharma, the Bhagavad-Gītā shines as a luminous jewel—resplendent with wisdom, sublime in its insight, and eternal in its relevance. It is not just a dialogue, but a profound revelation; it is not merely a scripture, but the voice of the Divine Himself.

Upon the sacred battlefield of Kurukṣetra, where dharma and adharma stand poised in dire opposition, the chariot of Arjuna becomes a sanctified seat of instruction. There—with the thunder of war in the distance and the weight of moral anguish in his heart—the warrior-disciple receives the timeless teachings from the Supreme Being: Bhagwāna Shri Krishna, the Jagadguru, whose every word carries the fragrance of truth and the thunder of transcendence.

From this consecrated setting, the Bhagavad-Gītā opens not as an abstract metaphysical treatise, but as the intimate cry of the human soul torn between duty and despair. Today we are at Chapter 16, so let us briefly recall where all we have been thus far in our Gītā journey.

— ॐ —

Chapter 1: Arjuna Viṣāda Yoga reveals the trembling heart of Arjuna, overcome by sorrow and compassion, confounded by the complexities of dharma. Here begins the spiritual journey—not in clarity, but in confusion; not with strength, but with the collapse of ego. His anguished refusal to fight becomes the fertile ground upon which the Lord sows the seeds of supreme knowledge.

Chapter 2: Sāṅkhya Yoga is the first full breath of that wisdom. Shri Krishna lifts Arjuna from his despair with the eternal truths of the self (Ātmā), teaching the imperishability of the soul, the nature of action, and the vision of the wise. This chapter is a gateway from lamentation to liberation, setting forth the vision of detached action and the equanimous sage.

Chapter 3: Karma Yoga delves deeper into the mystery of Karma-Yoga. The Lord unveils the path of duty performed without attachment to fruits—where ordained karmas become the means of inner purification and for performing worship of the Supreme.

Chapter 4: Jñāna-Karma-Saṃnyāsa Yoga introduces the sacredness of divine knowledge (jñāna) and the descending grace of the Lord through His avatāras. Krishna unveils His divinity, the eternal continuity of dharma, and the means of aligning one's action with divine intelligence.

Chapter 5: Karma-Saṃnyāsa Yoga explores the harmony between renunciation (saṃnyāsa) and selfless action, teaching that true renunciation lies not in the abandonment of action, but in the abandonment of desire.

Chapter 6: Dhyāna Yoga leads the seeker inward, toward the serene heights of meditation. The yogī who has mastered mind and senses dwells in union with the Self. This chapter marks a culmination of the earlier teachings on discipline, action, and equanimity, pointing toward the stillness of inner realization.

Having thus prepared Arjuna's intellect and heart, **Chapter 7: Jñāna-Vijñāna Yoga** opens a new vision of the Supreme Being—not as a mere philosophical principle, but as the all-pervading, all-sustaining Lord who is both the material and efficient cause of the cosmos.

Chapter 8: Akṣara-Brahma Yoga continues this exploration, revealing the eternal Braham, the mystery of death, and the paths of light and darkness that souls traverse. The chapter inspires the seeker to contemplate the Lord even at the hour of departure from the body.

Chapter 9: Rāja-Vidya Rāja-Guhya Yoga unveils the most exalted secret—the sovereignty of bhakti, the supremacy of devotion. The Lord speaks with unmatched tenderness of His nearness to all beings, of His readiness to accept even the smallest offering made with love.

Chapter 10: Vibhūti Yoga glorifies the divine opulences of the Lord that manifest throughout creation—wherever there is splendour, strength, beauty, or wisdom, it is but a spark of His infinite majesty.

Chapter 11: Viśvarūpa Darśana Yoga grants the climactic vision of the Universal Form—the cosmic Being in whom all worlds arise and dissolve. Arjuna beholds with awe and terror the grandeur of Krishna's all-encompassing divinity, and is thus forever transformed.

Chapter 12: Bhakti Yoga distils the Gītā's heart into the path of loving devotion. The Lord extols the devotee who worships with steadfast mind and selfless heart, assuring that He is easily attained by those who offer themselves wholly in love.

Chapter 13: Kṣetra-Kṣetrajña Vibhāga Yoga transitions into deeper metaphysics—discerning the body (kṣetra) and the knower of the body (kṣetrajña), and revealing the distinction between the mutable and the immutable, the perishable and the eternal.

Chapter 14: Guṇa-Traya Vibhāga Yoga illuminates the three guṇas—sattva, rajas, and tamas—that bind the soul to the cycle of birth and death. The aspirant is taught to rise above these qualities through knowledge and unwavering devotion.

Chapter 15: Puruṣottama Yoga presents the eternal aśvattha tree of saṃsāra, and reveals the Supreme Person—Puruṣottama—who transcends both the manifest and the unmanifest. The soul's true destiny is union with this Supreme Being beyond all duality.

And thusly we have arrived at **Chapter 16: Daivāsura Sampad Vibhāga Yoga**; and a new light is cast—this time, upon the moral and psychological forces within the human heart. The Lord now delineates the divine and demoniac tendencies that shape one's conduct, destiny, and proximity to the Supreme. The chapter is not merely ethical instruction; it is a mirror held up to the soul, challenging each seeker to discern the forces that uplift and those that degrade. It is a call to vigilance—of character, motive, and inner alignment—and a preparation for the concluding revelations.

In the chapters to come, the Gītā shall bring its teachings to culmination. **Chapter 17, Śraddhātraya Vibhāga Yoga,** explores the threefold division of faith, shedding light upon the subtle gradations in spiritual practice, while **Chapter 18, Mokṣa-Saṃnyāsa Yoga,** the grand finale, offers a majestic synthesis—uniting all previous paths in a final exhortation to surrender wholly unto the Divine. It is here that the Lord's voice echoes with boundless grace: "Consign all varieties of dharma unto Me. In Me alone is thy ultimate refuge."

— ॐ —

The journey of the Gītā is not linear but spiral—each teaching deepens the last, each vision refines the soul. As we enter the sixteenth chapter, we are called not merely to understand but to become—to let the divine qualities grow within, and to let the soul ascend toward its eternal source. Come now, let us listen with reverence, with stillness, and with a heart open to the Eternal Light.

ॐ Chapter Sixteen, A Bird's-Eye View

— ॐ तत सत ॐ —

Daivāsura-Sampad-Vibhāga Yoga

The sixteenth chapter of the Bhagavad-Gītā stands like a clear mirror, reflecting the dual tendencies that shape the destiny of all human beings. Entitled Daivāsura-Sampad-Vibhāga Yoga, "The Yoga of the Division between the Divine and Demoniac Endowments," it doesn't just describe outer conduct—it unveils the inner architecture of character that determines whether one ascends toward liberation or descends further into bondages.

At this stage of the sacred dialogue—having unveiled the nature of the Self, the Supreme Reality, the paths of action, devotion, and knowledge, and having illumined the world of the guṇas and the vast spectrum of faith and conduct—Shri Krishna now turns the seeker's gaze toward the moral and spiritual constitution of the soul.

— ॐ —

This chapter is not abstract ethics—it is spiritual anthropology. It lays bare the twofold heritage present in the heart of man: the **daivī sampad**, the divine qualities that lead to blessedness and freedom; and the **āsurī sampad**, the demoniac propensities that bind the soul to ignorance and suffering. The aim is not condemnation, but clarity; not judgment, but discernment.

The Lord, with luminous compassion, reveals how these inner qualities shape not only the outward life but also the ultimate destiny of the soul—toward the higher realms or into the darkness of rebirth. It is a call to vigilance, to introspection, and to the conscious cultivation of purity, truth, and fear of the Divine.

— ॐ —

Let us now briefly skim through the verses of this sacred chapter, verse by verse, so that our heart becomes attuned to the sublime instructions that will come our way.

Verses 1–3 open the chapter with a radiant enumeration of the divine qualities (daivī sampad)—fearlessness, purity of heart, steadfastness in knowledge, compassion, self-restraint, absence of pride, forgiveness, and devotion. These virtues, born of clarity and inner light, are the ornaments of the Sanātani soul who is aspiring towards liberation.

Verses 4–5 shift the gaze to the āsurī tendencies—the demoniac qualities such as hypocrisy, arrogance, harshness, ignorance, and cruelty. These traits are not only obstructions on the spiritual path but are the seeds that further our bondages. The Lord declares that the divine qualities lead to freedom, while the demoniac lead to degradation.

Verses 6–8 speak of the two types of beings—the divine and the demoniac—and describe the vision of those born under asuric influence—they who are deluded by materialism and deny the existence of truth and order in the universe. Believing the world to be without foundation, governed by desire alone, they embrace unrighteousness as their creed—and which is what describes the modern day world.

Verses 9–12 explore the surly ensnaring mode of life of such asuri beings — how, driven by insatiable desire, they pursue sensory enjoyment with reckless force. Caught in the web of endless craving, they remain bound in anxiety and fall deeper into the whirlpool of selfish ambition and deluded pride.

Verses 13–15 capture their inner boastfulness. "I am the doer; I am the enjoyer; there is none equal to me"—thus they speak, intoxicated by ego, power, and wealth. Blind to impermanence, they imagine themselves as invincible, untouched by karma or death.

Verse 16 shows the dark culmination of these tendencies—bewildered by many hopes, caught in a net of delusion, bound by desire, they plunge into unclean actions, losing sight of the Divine and the Self.

Verse 17 further reveals the traits of the demoniac—pride, arrogance, vanity, and harshness—all rooted in ignorance, devoid of humility or insight.

Verse 18 brings out their defiance: deluded by egotism, power, and lust, they despise the Lord who dwells in their own body and in others. Thus, they turn away from the indwelling Īśvara.

Verse 19 unveils the divine justice. Such beings, hateful and cruel, are cast repeatedly into demoniac wombs—lower births and darker realms—as a result of their unrighteous acts.

Verse 20 states with solemn gravity: "...the demoniac, caught in perpetual rebirth, do not attain Me, O Arjuna..." Ever lower they keep falling—birth upon birth, life after life—into realms bereft of truth and light.

Verse 21 now offers hope by revealing the portals to hell—lust, anger, and greed. These three consume the soul. The wise must abandon them utterly, for they are the path to ruin.

Verse 22 declares the way forward: He who escapes these three satanic gates, and lives according to śāstric guidance, walks the path of peace and ultimately attains the supreme goal.

Verse 23–24 conclude the chapter with a firm exhortation: the one who disregards the scriptural teachings and acts by his own impulse does not attain perfection, happiness, or the Supreme Goal. Therefore, the śāstra, the revealed word, must be the guiding light in determining right action and spiritual practice.

— ॐ —

With just 24 profound verses, thusly ends Chapter 16—a chapter of deep moral gravity and spiritual candour. This canto is both sword and balm—a sword that cuts through self-deception, and a balm that heals through clarity.

Here the Lord does not merely instruct; He awakens. For what is offered is not simply a map of virtue and vice—but a compass for the soul, pointing ever upward, toward the realm of the eternal, the divine, the free.

Now O mortal, let us listen well—for the divine charioteer Krishna speaks not only to Arjuna, but also directly to us -- to every soul caught between the pull of darkness and the call of light.

We Bow In Reverence To the Holy Bhagavad-Gitâ—
The Supreme-most Shastra which reveals:
Where the Âtmâ Shines, every Fear dissolves.

May our clarity rise.
May the three gates to Hell fall away for us.
May Gitâ-Yoga steady our heart.
May Gitâ-Dharma live through our every breath.
May the Supreme shine where we stand.
May Bhagwâna Shri Krishna guide our every step.
"I am the Âtmâ pure"—may we thusly ever remember our Self.

ॐ ॐ ॐ ॐ ॐ ॐ ॐ ॐ ॐ ॐ ॐ ॐ ॐ ॐ ॐ ॐ ॐ ॐ

षोडशोऽध्यायः - दैवासुरसम्पद्विभागयोगः

ṣoḍaśo'dhyāyaḥ - daivāsurasampadvibhāgayogaḥ

:: Canto – XVI ::

- Divine and Demoniacal Attributes –

ॐ ॐ ॐ ॐ ॐ ॐ ॐ ॐ ॐ ॐ ॐ ॐ ॐ ॐ ॐ ॐ ॐ ॐ

ॐ गीता श्लोकः १६.१ – GĪTĀ VERSE 16.1

ॐ श्रीमद्भगवद्गीतासूपनिषत्सु ब्रह्मविद्यायां योगशास्त्रे श्रीकृष्णार्जुनसंवादे
om śrīmadbhagavadgītāsūpaniṣatsu brahmavidyāyāṁ yogaśāstre śrīkṛṣṇārjunasaṁvāde
दैवासुरसम्पद्विभागयोगो नाम षोडशोऽध्यायः श्लोकः १
daivāsurasampadvibhāgayogo nāma ṣoḍaśo'dhyāyaḥ ślokaḥ 1

— ॐ —

श्रीभगवानुवाच --
śrībhagavānuvāca --

अभयं सत्त्वसंशुद्धिर्ज्ञानयोगव्यवस्थितिः ।
abhayaṁ sattvasaṁśuddhirjñānayogavyavasthitiḥ
दानं दमश्च यज्ञश्च स्वाध्यायस्तप आर्जवम् ॥ १६-१ ॥
dānaṁ damaśca yajñaśca svādhyāyastapa ārjavam (16-1)

Shri Bhagwāna said: **"Fearlessness, purity of heart, steadiness in the Yoga of Knowledge, and even so—charity, self-control, sacrifice, study of Vedas, austerity, uprightness; (16.1)**

—: *Word-by-Word* :—

श्रीभगवानुवाच śrī-bhagavān uvāca – The Blessed Lord said; **अभयम्** abhayam – fearlessness; **सत्त्वसंशुद्धिः** sattva-saṁśuddhiḥ – purity of mind; **ज्ञानयोगव्यवस्थितिः** jñāna-yoga-vyavasthitiḥ – steadfastness in the path of knowledge and yoga; **दानम्** dānam – charity; **दमः** damaḥ – self-restraint; **च** ca – and; **यज्ञः** yajñaḥ – Yajna (sacrifice); **स्वाध्यायः** svādhyāyaḥ – study of the scriptures; **तपः** tapaḥ – austerity; **आर्जवम्** ārjavam – straightforwardness.

—: *Understanding The Verse* :—

— ॐ श्रीकृष्णाय नमः ॐ —

Out of His infinite compassion and wisdom, Bhagwāna Shri Krishna commences a profound delineation of the divine qualities beginning with this luminous verse. These godly qualities—belonging to those endowed with the divine nature (**दैवी सम्पदा** daivī-sampadāḥ)—are enumerated from verses 16.1 through 16.3. These are qualities that illuminate the path to the eventual emancipation of the soul.

— o —

Verse 16.1 lists the first nine endowments: (1) fearlessness (अभयं abhayaṁ); (2) purity of heart (सत्त्वसंशुद्धिः sattva-saṁśuddhiḥ); (3) steadfastness in knowledge and yoga (ज्ञानयोगव्यवस्थितिः jñāna-yoga-vyavasthitiḥ); (4) charity (दानम् dānam); (5) self-control (दमः damaḥ); (6) sacrifice (यज्ञः yajñaḥ); (7) study of the scriptures (स्वाध्यायः svādhyāyaḥ); (8) austerity (तपः tapaḥ); and (9) uprightness (आर्जवम् ārjavam).

— o —

Verse 16.2 continues with the next eleven: (10) non-violence (अहिंसा ahiṁsā); (11) truthfulness (सत्यम् satyam); (12) absence of anger (अक्रोधः akrodhaḥ); (13) renunciation or spirit of sacrifice (त्यागः tyāgaḥ); (14) serenity (शान्तिः śāntiḥ); (15) absence of slander (अपैशुनम् apaiśunam); (16) compassion for all beings (दया भूतेषु dayā bhūteṣu); (17) non-covetousness (अलोलुप्त्वम् aloluptvam); (18) gentleness (मार्दवम् mārdavam); (19) modesty (ह्रीः hrīḥ); and (20) steadiness or freedom from fickleness (अचापलम् acāpalam).

— o —

Verse 16.3 concludes with the final six divine qualities: (21) vigor or spiritual splendor (तेजः tejaḥ); (22) forgiveness (क्षमा kṣamā); (23) fortitude (धृतिः dhṛtiḥ); (24) purity inward and outward (शौचम् śaucam); (25) absence of malice (अद्रोहः adrohaḥ); and (26) humility or absence of conceit (नातिमानिता nātimānitā).

— o —

Together, these twenty-six qualities constitute the daivī-sampadāḥ, the natural marks of those born with divine endowment— guiding them toward liberation and harmony with the eternal truth.

These three verses stand as the threshold to a deeper discourse on the inherent dualities which govern human nature: the divine and the demoniac, the elevating and the binding.

— ॐ श्रीरामाय नमः ॐ —

Shri Bhagwāna begins Verse 16.1 enumerating the virtues that serve as the very bedrock of a seeker's ascent toward the Supreme. These are: •fearlessness born of wisdom; •purity of heart unsullied by selfish motive; •steadfastness in the arduous discipline of Jñāna-Yoga; •charity performed with a pure heart; •restraint over the senses; •austerity that fortifies the spirit; •study of the sacred Vedas that nourishes discernment; •and unwavering uprightness in thought, word, and deed.

These qualities are not just ethical exhortations but are profound inner transformations that harmonize the aspirant with the eternal ऋत ṛta—the cosmic order.

Each virtue mentioned is a gateway, leading the soul from the entanglements of संसार saṁsāra toward the serene heights of self-realization. The verse, therefore, serves as both a mirror and a map: reflecting the ideal state of divine excellence and guiding the aspirant in cultivating these luminous attributes through disciplined spiritual practice and inner purification.

—: Key Sanskrit Terms :—

— ॐ तत सत ॐ —

Come now, let us trace the silver thread of meaning through the verse, where each Sanskrit word glimmers like pearls upon the still waters of thought. Let us hear the Sanskrit as a new dawn breaking clear. Fearlessness, purity, steadfastness—each syllable is a bright flame of divine quality.

— ॐ —

अभयम् (Abhayam) – Fearlessness:
Derived from the root भी "bhī" (to fear) with the negating prefix अ "a-," abhayam denotes not mere recklessness, but the absence of existential fear born from the realization of the Self (ātma-jñāna). It is the courage that arises when the जीव jīva understands its eternal nature, untouched by death or sorrow.

— ॐ —

सत्त्वसंशुद्धिः (Sattva-saṁśuddhiḥ) – Purity of being (or of heart):
सत्त्व Sattva—the luminous, harmonious quality among the three guṇas —refers to clarity, serenity, and truthfulness in thought, emotion, and intention.
It indicates the refinement of inner consciousness, free from malice, deceit, and agitation.
It is our awareness become purified (संशुद्धिः saṁśuddhiḥ);

— ॐ —

ज्ञानयोगव्यवस्थितिः (Jñāna-yoga-vyavasthitiḥ) – Steadfastness in the Yoga of Knowledge:
ज्ञानयोग Jñāna-yoga is the path of discernment between the Real (सत sat) and the Unreal (असत asat), culminating in Self-realization.

व्यवस्थितिः Vyavasthitiḥ implies steadfast abidance — not merely theoretical engagement, but profound inner absorption in the inquiry of Braham, transcending fleeting identifications.

— ॐ —

दानम् (Dānam) – Charity or Giving:

More than material offering, दान dāna symbolizes the relinquishment of possessiveness ममता (mamatā) and ego अहंकार (ahaṅkāra)—an outward expression of inward detachment.

At a deeper level, it reflects the understanding that the entire cosmos is pervaded by ईश्वर Īśvara (—so what really is mine?)

— ॐ —

दमः (Damaḥ) – Restraint of the senses:

A crucial शान्ति कारक śānti-karaka (peace-bringing discipline), दम dama refers to control over the external sense organs.

It is the check placed on outward cravings, a necessary foundation for meditation and Self-inquiry.

— ॐ —

यज्ञः (Yajñaḥ) – Sacrifice or Sacred Offering:

Not merely the fire rituals, यज्ञ yajña embodies any act consecrated to the Divine without selfish motive—the only motive being serving Sanātana-Dharma in obedience to Bhagwāna Shri Krishna.

All duties, when surrendered as offerings to Braham—whose manifest form is Krishna—become yajña.

This यज्ञः also includes the inner yajña of surrendering the ego.

— ॐ —

स्वाध्यायः (Svādhyāyaḥ) – Study of the Self through the Vedas:

स्वाध्याय svādhyāya is the reverent recitation and contemplation of श्रुति śruti (revealed texts).

It aligns the intellect (buddhi) with ऋत ṛta (cosmic order) and illumines the path of jñāna.

स्वाध्याय svādhyāya is both discipline and devotion.

— ॐ —

तपः (Tapaḥ) – Austerity:

From the root तप "tap" (to burn), it refers to disciplines that purify the inner being.

तपः Tapaḥ burns away impurities मल (mala), revealing the inner radiance of the Self.

— ॐ —

आर्जवम् (Ārjavam) – Simplicity / Uprightness:

Sincerity, absence of duplicity, and unity of thought, word, and deed — आर्जव ārjava is inner integrity. It is the straight path wherein the soul walks uncloaked, unmasked, and unafraid.

—: In Brief :—

— ॐ श्रीकृष्णाय नमः ॐ —

Thus, in this opening declaration of Chapter 16, the Lord sets forth the hallmarks of the divine nature—virtues that collectively form a tapestry of सात्त्विक sāttvika strength and spiritual integrity.

These attributes are not to be viewed in isolation but as interwoven threads that, together, refine and elevate the consciousness of the aspirant.

The fearless heart arises from the clear vision of the Self; purity is the natural fragrance of a mind detached from worldly cravings; steadfastness in wisdom and Yoga anchors the aspirant amid life's storms.

Charity, self-restraint, austerity, and scriptural study—they all sustain our progress, ensuring that the inner light remains undimmed.

— ॐ अग्निजन्मने नमः ॐ —

The verse subtly reminds us that true spiritual progress is a harmonious blending of jnāna, karma, bhakti—knowledge, action, and devotion—all grounded in purity and unwavering rectitude.

Having laid out the divine virtues, the Lord prepares, in the verses which follow, to contrast them with the आसुरी सम्पदा āsurī sampadā—the qualities that entangle the soul in bondage and delusion.

This verse stands not only as an inspiring ideal but as a preparatory prelude, sharpening the seeker's discernment to recognize the opposing forces within—and thereby to consciously choose the path that leads to liberation, which alone is the goal of human life.

— ॐ तत सत ॐ —

Before we move on, let us bow in reverence to this sacred verse. Write it by hand, reflect on its meaning, chant it aloud, make it your own.

— ॐ —

श्रीभगवानुवाच --
śrībhagavānuvāca --
अभयं सत्त्वसंशुद्धिर्ज्ञानयोगव्यवस्थितिः ।
abhayaṁ sattvasaṁśuddhirjñānayogavyavasthitiḥ
दानं दमश्च यज्ञश्च स्वाध्यायस्तप आर्जवम् ॥ १६-१ ॥
dānaṁ damaśca yajñaśca svādhyāyastapa ārjavam (16-1)

ॐ

श्रीभगवानुवाच -- śrībhagavānuvāca --

अभयं सत्त्वसंशुद्धिर्ज्ञानयोगव्यवस्थितिः ।

abhayaṁ sattvasaṁśuddhirjñānayogavyavasthitiḥ

दानं दमश्च यज्ञश्च स्वाध्यायस्तप आर्जवम् ॥ १६-१ ॥

dānaṁ damaśca yajñaśca svādhyāyastapa ārjavam (16-1)

ॐ तत्सदिति श्रीमद्भगवद्गीतासूपनिषत्सु ब्रह्मविद्यायां योगशास्त्रे श्रीकृष्णार्जुनसंवादे

om tatsaditi śrīmadbhagavadgītāsūpaniṣatsu brahmavidyāyāṁ yogaśāstre śrīkṛṣṇārjunasaṁvāde

दैवासुरसम्पद्विभागयोगो नाम षोडशोऽध्यायः श्लोकः १

daivāsurasampadvibhāgayogo nāma ṣoḍaśo'dhyāyaḥ ślokaḥ 1

Om-Tat-Sat—Om (Braham) is the sole Reality. In the Yogic Scripture on the Science-of-Braham, the Shrimada-Bhāgvada-Gītā Upanishad, we hereby conclude Shloka 1 of the Dialogue between Shrī Krishna and Arjuna entitled Daivāsura-Sampada-Vibhāga-Yoga, Canto XVI.

Canto-Sixteen begins with अभयं Fearlessness

And whence the Seed of अभयं Fearlessness?—It's in Oneness.

Wherefrom arise these trembling shades?
This whispering/whimpering phantom called Fear?
'Tis born of Twoness, of Duality:
A sundering veil betwixt Self and the Seer—
betwixt Seer and the Seen
betwixt the Self and the Other—these helter-skelter scenes.

Whereas

In the womb of Oneness—where Braham breathes—no other besides,
There lies the rootless tree of Courage, where naught from Truth can hide—for naught exists other than that Oneness..

O child of the Infinite Flame, these shivers are not thine own—
But of a Deluded-Dreamer lost in names, far from his true Home:
Which Home is That Boundless Throne of Oneness: Braham.

तत् त्वम् असि tat-tvam-asi—Know Thou art That—
Eternal, Pure—where fear hath no body, no repose.
In the silence of Oneness, rises bold a lotus called the Âtmâ—
with none to love, hate, fear, oppose.
One breath within Braham—
And the storm of tremblings ceases right there and then.

ॐ गीता श्लोकः १६.२ – GĪTĀ VERSE 16.2

ॐ श्रीमद्भगवद्गीतासूपनिषत्सु ब्रह्मविद्यायां योगशास्त्रे श्रीकृष्णार्जुनसंवादे
om śrīmadbhagavadgītāsūpaniṣatsu brahmavidyāyāṁ yogaśāstre śrīkṛṣṇārjunasaṁvāde
दैवासुरसम्पद्विभागयोगो नाम षोडशोऽध्यायः श्लोकः २
daivāsurasampadvibhāgayogo nāma ṣoḍaśo'dhyāyaḥ ślokaḥ 2

— ॐ —

अहिंसा सत्यमक्रोधस्त्यागः शान्तिरपैशुनम् ।
ahiṁsā satyamakrodhastyāgaḥ śāntirapaiśunam
दया भूतेष्वलोलुप्त्वं मार्दवं ह्रीरचापलम् ॥१६-२॥
dayā bhūteṣvaloluptvaṁ mārdavaṁ hrīracāpalam (16-2)

non-injury, truthfulness, absence of anger, self-sacrifice, quietude, composure of mind, abstention from slander, compassion towards beings, non-covetousness, gentleness, modesty, refraining from frivolous pursuits; (16.2)

—: Word-by-Word :—

अहिंसा ahiṁsā – non-violence; **सत्यम्** satyam – truthfulness; **अक्रोधः** akrodhaḥ – absence of anger; **त्यागः** tyāgaḥ – renunciation; **शान्तिः** śāntiḥ – tranquility; **अपैशुनम्** apaiśunam – absence of malice; **दया** dayā – compassion; **भूतेषु** bhūteṣu – toward all beings; **अलोलुप्त्वम्** aloluptvam – absence of greed; **मार्दवम्** mārdavam – gentleness; **ह्रीः** hrīḥ – modesty; **अचापलम्** acāpalam – absence of fickleness.

—: Understanding The Verse :—

— ॐ श्रीकृष्णाय नमः ॐ —

In this profound verse Shri Krishna unfolds a luminous array of virtues that adorn the soul inclined towards the path of righteousness and divine realization.

The noble qualities—**अहिंसा** ahiṁsā (non-injury), **सत्यम्** satyam (truthfulness), **अक्रोध** akrodha (absence of anger), **त्याग** tyāga (renunciation), **शान्ति** śānti (quietude), and others—form a garland of sublime attributes that not only refine personal character but also harmonize one's existence with the cosmic order, **ऋत** ṛta.

— ॐ भक्तप्रियाय नमः ॐ —

Each virtue is not just an outer observance—sometimes an external show designed to fool ourselves and the world and hopefully gods as well—but an inward flowering of purity and restraint -- requiring the aspirant to embody these ideals innately: in thought, word, and deed.

These attributes are luminous symbols of deeper spiritual laws, woven into the very fabric of the eternal Sanātana-Dharma.

They serve as guideposts on the arduous journey of self-mastery and transcendence, enabling us to rise above the turbulence of lower impulses and abide in the serene equipoise of the Self.

This verse is a contemplative mirror, inviting us to measure our progress in aligning with Sanātana-Dharma's eternal pulse;

and as we traverse these qualities, we begin to glimpse the essence of what it means to live as an instrument of Krishna, of His Divine Will—moving from self-centeredness to selflessness—which comprises of taking to Gītā-Dharma—and which then takes us from the worldly restlessness to the ocean of abiding peace within our Self.

—: Key Sanskrit Terms :—

— ॐ तत सत ॐ —

Now let us meander along the verse's inner pathways, pausing to behold its Sanskrit phrases—where thought ripens into vision and language becomes light.

Lo, the words here linger like cool water upon the heart: non-violence, truth, absence of anger—each word soothing, cleansing, serene.

— ॐ —

अहिंसा (Ahiṁsā) – Non-injury:

From the root हिंस "hiṁs" meaning to harm, अहिंसा ahiṁsā is its direct negation.

Yet, this is no passive non-violence—it is active benevolence. It springs not from timidity but from the realization that all beings are आत्मवत ātmavat, endowed with the same essence.

To harm another is to harm our own Self—a result of ignorance.

Mind it this is not the surficial pretentious 'non-injury' अहिंसा ahiṁsā that is bandied about in the modern world—happily succumbing to wickedness, vice, evilness of the adharmic asuras closing your eyes.

Bhagwāna Krishna's exhortation to Arjuna: "Slay this enemy that stands before thee in the shape of adharma"—is the silent refrain that is implicit in all the teachings of Gītā-Dharma. Non-violence can come only from first recognizing the strength of the Self.

— ॐ —

सत्यं (Satyam) – Truthfulness:

सत्यं Satyam is more than verbal honesty—it is alignment with ऋत ṛta, the cosmic truth.

It is speech, thought, and action rooted in परमार्थ paramārtha (the Supreme Reality), not merely factual correctness.

As the Muṇḍaka Upaniṣad declares, सत्यम् एव जयते "Satyameva jayate"—truth alone triumphs.

सत्यमेव जयते नानृतं जयति सत्येन पन्था विततो देवयानः । येनाक्रमन्त्यृषयो ह्याप्तकामा, यत्र तत्सत्यस्य परमं निधानम्

Truth alone wins, and not untruth. By truth is laid the path called Devayana, by which the desireless seers ascend to where exists the supreme treasure attainable through truth. [mundakopanishad-U 3.1.6]

— ॐ —

अक्रोधः (Akrodhaḥ) – Absence of Anger:

क्रोध Krodha arises from unfulfilled desire काम (kāma);

and its negation, अक्रोध akrodha, is cessation of anger—reflecting a mastery over the emotional tides of the mind.

It is the serenity that flows from inner fullness, wherein nothing external has the power to disturb.

— ॐ —

त्यागः (Tyāgaḥ) – Renunciation:

Not mere abandonment of action, but the relinquishment of attachment to the fruits फल त्याग (phala-tyāga).

True त्याग tyāga is internal—it is freedom from possessiveness, the offering of all acts into the fire of the Divine.

— ॐ —

शान्तिः (Śāntiḥ) – Inner Peace:

शान्ति Śānti is not silence enforced by exhaustion, but the luminous stillness of the mind established in the Self.

It is the peace that surpasses all external stimuli—unshaken by gain or loss, praise or blame.

— ॐ —

अपैशुनम् (Apaiśunam) – Absence of Slander:

The restraint from speaking ill of others, even in their absence.

पैशुनम् Paiśunam is rooted in ego and comparison;

अपैशुनम् apaiśunam is the noble silence of one who sees the same Self (Ātmā) in all.

— ॐ —

दया भूतेषु (Dayā Bhūteṣu) – Compassion toward all beings:

दया Dayā is not pity—it is empathetic resonance with the joys and sorrows of all beings.

भूतेषु Bhūteṣu includes not only humans but all living entities—for each and every being and thing is conscious and has a soul.

This universal compassion arises naturally from Self-knowledge—the knowledge of oneness: that all is the One-Existence satt-chitt-ānanda braham, whose manifest form is Bhagwāna Shri Krishna.

— ॐ —

अलोलुप्त्वम् (Aloluptvam) – Non-covetousness:

From the root लुप् "lup" (to covet), this negation reflects non-attachment to sense pleasures.

अलोलुप्त्वम् Aloluptvam is inner contentment संतुष्टि (santuṣṭi)—whereby the mind is no longer disturbed by cravings for acquisition. It is वैराग्य Vairagya.

— ॐ —

मार्दवम् (Mārdavam) – Gentleness:

A quality of softness in speech, action, and presence.

It is born of humility and love, a reflection of inner refinement संस्कार (samskāra) and a heart untouched by pride.

It all emerges naturally when man realizes who-I-am.

— ॐ —

ह्रीः (Hrīḥ) – Modesty / Sense of shame:

This is not social awkwardness, but the noble inner restraint which holds one back from ignoble acts;

ह्रीः Hrīḥ is the spiritual dignity आत्म-गौरव (ātma-gaurava) that arises from awareness of the Self's divinity and sanctity;

it arises naturally from realizing one's divine nature, of one's grandness, honor, pureness as the Ātmā—and realizing that indulging in this lowlife act is unbecoming of me.

— ॐ —

अचापलम् (Acāpalam) – Freedom from frivolity or restlessness:

चपल Capala is outward agitation, the fluttering of the mind through speech and deeds.

अचापलम् Acāpalam is the natural composure स्तिथि (sthiti) of one whose consciousness abides steadily in the Self.

—: In Brief :—

— ॐ श्रीकृष्णाय नमः ॐ —

Thus, through the meticulous enumeration of these sacred attributes, Bhagwāna Shri Krishna delineates the essential features of a divinely endowed nature—a temperament suffused with sattva and attuned to the highest good.

Each virtue, whether it be the gentleness of demeanor or the steadfastness of inner quietude, serves as a means to the ultimate purification of the mind and heart—gradually dissolving the veils of ignorance and egoity that enslave thee.

The verse underscores that such qualities are not superficial embellishments but are integral to the unfoldment of true wisdom (jñāna) and dispassion (vairāgya), paving the way to Mokṣa—the final release from worldly bondages.

— ॐ श्रीरामाय नमः ॐ —

Though these virtues may seem simple when listed, their deep-rooted practice requires vigilant self-awareness and unwavering commitment. They are both the fruit of prior spiritual maturity and the seeds of future spiritual blossoming.

In this way, the verse serves as a sacred touchstone—urging us aspirant to live a life of inner harmony, ethical integrity, and divine alignment.

As we proceed to the next verse, Shri Krishna brings this exploration of दैवी सम्पदा daivī-sampad (divine qualities) toward its culmination, offering a more complete vision of the character and destiny of those who embody these virtues fully.

Thus, the teaching gently leads us from the listing of individual qualities to the larger understanding of their place within the grand cosmic order and the soul's eternal journey.

— ॐ तत सत ॐ —

Before moving on, let us once more bow in deep reverence before this sacred verse of the Bhagavad-Gītā, an eternal beacon of wisdom that ceaselessly illumines the path of seekers. Engage with its form—inscribe it with your own hand, let your heart dwell upon its meaning, and raise your voice in its chanting—for within these syllables echoes the undying proclamation delivered millennia ago on the battlefield of Kurukshetra. These words, transmitted unchanged across the unbroken chain of generations, form a living bridge, linking us to that sanctified era when Bhagwāna Shri Krishna Himself walked this earth and bestowed this divine teaching. Through the luminous vibration of these sacred Sanskrit sounds, we are drawn nearer to His timeless presence, touching the very heartbeat of the Eternal.

— ॐ —

अहिंसा सत्यमक्रोधस्त्यागः शान्तिरपैशुनम् ।
ahiṁsā satyamakrodhastyāgaḥ śāntirapaiśunam
दया भूतेष्वलोलुप्त्वं मार्दवं ह्रीरचापलम् ॥ १६-२ ॥
dayā bhūteṣvaloluptvaṁ mārdavaṁ hrīracāpalam (16-2)

अहिंसा सत्यमक्रोधस्त्यागः शान्तिरपैशुनम् ।
ahiṁsā satyamakrodhastyāgaḥ śāntirapaiśunam
दया भूतेष्वलोलुप्त्वं मार्दवं ह्रीरचापलम् ॥ १६-२ ॥
dayā bhūteṣvaloluptvaṁ mārdavaṁ hrīracāpalam (16-2)

ॐ तत्सदिति श्रीमद्भगवद्गीतासूपनिषत्सु ब्रह्मविद्यायां योगशास्त्रे श्रीकृष्णार्जुनसंवादे
om tatsaditi śrīmadbhagavadgītāsūpaniṣatsu brahmavidyāyāṁ yogaśāstre śrīkṛṣṇārjunasaṁvāde
दैवासुरसम्पद्विभागयोगो नाम षोडशोऽध्यायः श्लोकः २
daivāsurasampadvibhāgayogo nāma ṣoḍaśo'dhyāyaḥ ślokaḥ 2

Om-Tat-Sat—Om (Braham) is the sole Reality. In the Yogic Scripture on the Science-of-Braham, the Shrimada-Bhāgvada-Gītā Upanishad, we hereby conclude Shloka 2 of the Dialogue between Shrī Krishna and Arjuna entitled Daivāsura-Sampada-Vibhāga-Yoga, Canto XVI.

The One Self in All

With eyes of wisdom open wide—all shrouds removed / unveiled,
The sage perceives One-Light in all—no creatures made to grieve.

From Braham have sprung all these forms—all are but single breath,
Who kills to eat another one—just strikes himself to death.

No "other" walks the forest vast, no stranger fills the field,
For all are threads within one cloth—by sacred Dharma sealed.

What harm can come when none is foe, when none is truly two?
When Self beholds the Self in All—no violence can ensue.

Remember: Ahimsā अहिंसा naturally blooms —
where Sanâtana-Dharma's non-dual flame illumines all that we do.

But the Modern-Day Practicality is So Different

He talks God, religion, kindness, love—while greedily guttling beef,
The brute kills the motherly cow to eat—
after first robbing her milk -- to nourish himself and his kids.

Unto him—the malich asura—kindness is an antique flaw,
Peace शान्तिः to him is cowardice.
His very presence is now toxic; and he ends up wounding,
Even with a very simple glance, of his knife-sharp eyes,

Mocking non-injury, he kills to profit in self-made wars.
He drives his knife a little more deep—with every pat, on thy back.

He steps over the fallen natch, believing that he only climbs,
Lo behold the "modern" man—who calls himself ostensibly civilized.

ॐ गीता श्लोकः १६.३ – GĪTĀ VERSE 16.3

ॐ श्रीमद्भगवद्गीतासूपनिषत्सु ब्रह्मविद्यायां योगशास्त्रे श्रीकृष्णार्जुनसंवादे
om śrīmadbhagavadgītāsūpaniṣatsu brahmavidyāyāṁ yogaśāstre śrīkṛṣṇārjunasaṁvāde
दैवासुरसम्पद्विभागयोगो नाम षोडशोऽध्यायः श्लोकः ३
daivāsurasampadvibhāgayogo nāma ṣoḍaśo'dhyāyaḥ ślokaḥ 3

— ॐ —

तेजः क्षमा धृतिः शौचमद्रोहो नातिमानिता ।
tejaḥ kṣamā dhṛtiḥ śaucamadroho nātimānitā
भवन्ति सम्पदं दैवीमभिजातस्य भारत ॥१६-३॥
bhavanti sampadaṁ daivīmabhijātasya bhārata (16-3)

sublimity, forgiveness, fortitude, purity, absence of hatred and conceit—these are the marks of one born of Divine endowments, O Bhārata. (16.3)

—: Word-by-Word :—

तेजः tejaḥ – vigor; **क्षमा** kṣamā – forgiveness; **धृतिः** dhṛtiḥ – fortitude; **शौचम्** śaucam – cleanliness; **अद्रोहः** adrohaḥ – absence of malice; **नातिमानिता** nātimānitā – absence of excessive pride; **भवन्ति** bhavanti – are; **सम्पदम्** sampadam – the qualities; **दैवीम्** daivīm – divine; **अभिजातस्य** abhijātasya – born of; **भारत** bhārata – O descendant of Bharata.

—: Understanding The Verse :—

— ॐ श्रीकृष्णाय नमः ॐ —

We now enter the luminous precincts of Bhagavad-Gītā 16.3, beholding the final jewel in the triad of verses which outline the दैवी-म्पदा daivī-sampadā—the divine endowments. The Lord, in His infinite compassion, does not merely instruct our mind but calls out to our soul—invoking the remembrance of its innate स्वभाव svabhāva, its eternal and pristine essence. Here we are invited once more to reflect deeply on the tapestry of virtues marking the Path of Light.

— ॐ खरदूषणहन्त्रे नमः ॐ —

Bhagwāna Shri Krishna here further delineates with crystalline clarity further attributes of the daivī nature: •grandeur of spirit तेजः (tejaḥ); •patience and forgiveness क्षमा (kṣamā); •resolute endurance धृतिः (dhṛti); •inner and outer purity शौचम् (śaucam); •the absence of hostility अद्रोहः (adroha); and •freedom from vanity or pride नातिमानिता (nā-atimānitā).

Together, these qualities form the culmination of the divine virtues, painting a complete portrait of the one attuned to dharma and fit for the path of emancipation. Each quality here is not an isolated ornament but an expression of a harmonized inner life—a life where lower instincts have been transcended and the soul abides in alignment with the cosmic order. We shall contemplate these virtues not merely as ethical ideals but as transformative forces, potent in their capacity to forge a character worthy of the Divine's nearness and grace.

—: Key Sanskrit Terms :—

— ॐ तत सत ॐ —

Come now, let us rest with the Sanskrit as with a garland of virtues strung—compassion, gentleness, modesty—each syllable a blossom fragrant, soft. Let us hold the Sanskrit terms up to the light, and observe how they refract meaning—how each word casts its own shadow, its own gleam. As its facets unfold, the verse begins to breathe like a hidden flower opening at dawn—no longer thought alone, but virtues shimmering into life. Each trait glimmers like a rare jewel of the soul, casting its hue upon the inner chambers of the heart. Let the verse moves within us—to weave that quiet enchantment by which the pathway of Dharma becomes revealed.

— ॐ —

तेजः (Tejaḥ) – Sublimity / Divine radiance:

This is not mere external brilliance, but the inner spiritual effulgence born naturally of truth, clarity, and steadfastness in dharma.

तेज Tejas is the glow of jñāna, the fire of discrimination (viveka), and the invincible moral force that arises from purity.

— ॐ —

क्षमा (Kṣamā) – Forbearance / Forgiveness:

This is not weakness, but the strength of one who is unmoved by provocation.

क्षमा Kṣamā arises from the understanding: "Who really is there to forgive, to take the high moral ground—when all are merely appearances within Braham?" It is a noble endurance even of insults—without inner disturbance.

However, those in grahastha-āshrama should make a pretence at harshness and anger—to maintain order, or else the societal order itself will crumble away over time. But let the fire stay on the outside—it should never reach the heart.

— ॐ —

धृतिः (Dhṛtiḥ) – Fortitude / Steadfastness:

Derived from the root धृ "dhṛ" (to hold), it is the resolute endurance through trials.

धृतिः Dhṛtiḥ is the anchoring of the mind in the true Self—the higher Self, even amid storms.

It reflects deep inner maturity, where faith in one's dharma never wavers.

— ॐ —

शौचम् (Śaucam) – Purity:

This is twofold—external cleanliness and internal clarity.

अन्तः शुद्धि Antaḥ-śuddhi, or purity of motive, thought, and desire, is especially stressed in Vedānta.

Without शौचम् śaucam, jñāna cannot take root.

— ॐ —

अद्रोहः (Adrohaḥ) – Absence of Malice / Harmlessness:

द्रोह Droha implies treachery or ill-will, often subtle and hidden.

अद्रोहः Adrohaḥ is the complete absence of that sentiment—a natural outgrowth of the vision of oneness.

It is not mere tolerance, but the innate bliss of the Self, in which all extraneous—friend, foe etc., considerations—lose meanings.

— ॐ —

नातिमानिता (Nātimānitā) – Absence of excessive pride:

मानिता Mānitā is the sense of self-importance and अतिमानिता ātimānitā is its hyperbole. And now the prefix न "na-" negates it all. Even the seed of such conceit is not there.

नातिमानिता Nātimānitā is the humility born not of self-belittlement, but of the realization that "I am not this ego—I am the witness, the Self."

— ॐ —

संपदं दैवीम् (Sampadaṁ Daivīm) – Divine endowment:

संपद Sampad implies a wealth, an inner treasure.

दैवी Daivī indicates it is not mundane but of divine origin.

These qualities are the natural fragrance of the Ātmā— which start blossoming under the gentle light of Gītā-Dharma.

— ॐ —

अभिजातस्य (Abhijātasya) – Of one who is born with / inclined towards:

अभिजात Abhijāta signifies noble birth, but here it implies spiritual inclination, a soul matured through संस्कार saṁskāras and prior जन्म janmas (births), who is predisposed toward मुक्ति mukti.

— ॐ —

भारत (Bhārata) – O scion of the Bharata lineage:

An address rich with invocation. By calling Arjuna भारत "Bhārata," Shri Krishna reminds him of his noble dharmic lineage, charging him to rise to the stature of the great ṛṣis and kṣatriyas who lived for righteousness.

—: In Brief :—

— ॐ श्रीकृष्णाय नमः ॐ —

In this verse, the Lord completes His enumeration of the दैवी सम्पदा daivī-sampadā, the divine virtues that adorn the soul on its ascent to spiritual freedom.

The term 'Daivī Sampad' encapsulates these exalted qualities—virtues that, whether innate or cultivated through sincere practice, are the true treasures of a seeker who aspires toward God-Realization.

Such qualities—whether it be the sublime energy that fuels righteous action, the steadfast endurance that holds fast amidst trials, or the humility that dissolves the ego—are radiant signs of a soul that has been graced with divine gifts.

— ॐ पूर्वभाषिणे नमः ॐ —

Through these virtues, the seeker is gradually purified, becoming a vessel through which the light of dharma can shine unobstructed.

Mind it: these are not mere ethical prescriptions but living manifestations of divine nature (Daivī Prakṛti) itself, essential for spiritual maturity and for abiding in the supreme peace that transcends all worldly entanglements.

— ॐ अग्निजन्मने नमः ॐ —

Having thus described in these three verses the marks of the one endowed with divine nature—qualities that are ever worthy of being embraced and cultivated—the Lord next turns His gaze to the other side of the spiritual spectrum.

In the forthcoming verses, Shri Krishna will unveil the characteristics of the demoniac आसुरी (āsuric) nature, cautioning us against the snares of those destructive tendencies which, if left unchecked, bind the soul deeper into the vicious cycle of ignorance and suffering. Thus, the sacred dialogue shifts from the luminous to the shadowed—offering a holistic vision of the forces at play within human hearts.

— ॐ तत सत ॐ —

Before we move on, let us bow in reverence to this sacred verse. Write it by hand, reflect on its meaning, chant it aloud, make it your own.

— ॐ —

तेजः क्षमा धृतिः शौचमद्रोहो नातिमानिता ।
tejaḥ kṣamā dhṛtiḥ śaucamadroho nātimānitā
भवन्ति सम्पदं दैवीमभिजातस्य भारत ॥१६-३॥
bhavanti sampadaṁ daivīmabhijātasya bhārata (16-3)

— ॐ —

तेजः क्षमा धृतिः शौचमद्रोहो नातिमानिता ।
tejaḥ kṣamā dhṛtiḥ śaucamadroho nātimānitā
भवन्ति सम्पदं दैवीमभिजातस्य भारत ॥१६-३॥
bhavanti sampadaṁ daivīmabhijātasya bhārata (16-3)

ॐ तत्सदिति श्रीमद्भगवद्गीतासूपनिषत्सु ब्रह्मविद्यायां योगशास्त्रे श्रीकृष्णार्जुनसंवादे
om tatsaditi śrīmadbhagavadgītāsūpaniṣatsu brahmavidyāyāṁ yogaśāstre śrīkṛṣṇārjunasaṁvāde
दैवासुरसम्पद्विभागयोगो नाम षोडशोऽध्यायः श्लोकः ३
daivāsurasampadvibhāgayogo nāma ṣoḍaśo'dhyāyaḥ ślokaḥ 3

Om-Tat-Sat—Om (Braham) is the sole Reality. In the Yogic Scripture on the Science-of-Braham, the Shrimada-Bhāgvada-Gītā Upanishad, we hereby conclude Shloka 3 of the Dialogue between Shrī Krishna and Arjuna entitled Daivāsura-Sampada-Vibhāga-Yoga, Canto XVI.

I See the Shining Flame, But alas, it a'int Not yet Mine!

O me, I read the list of sacred traits—
तेजः क्षमा... Tejah, kshama... and feel both awe and ache.
Where is that light in me that burns—yet does not scorch?
Where the within fire—which does not harm?

Forgiveness?

Aye, I do speak the gentle word,
Yet inwardly I smolder with every old wrong done.
I hold grudges like relics,
Holding them sacred—even when they have rotted over time.

Fortitude?

Nay, I need quick rewards—have no patience for patience.
I love walking only on dandy roads that are always sunlit—
And when shadows fall, I do cry and rage—I have to admit.

That strength which waits with calm midst all storms,
It is not yet in my breath — just only a wish for now.
Aye, I do see the flame, the Sunlit दैवी daivi road—
But I walk still as my former weak-selfish shadow.
Perhaps one day by Krishna's grace... things will turn around.

ॐ गीता श्लोकः १६.४ – GĪTĀ VERSE 16.4

ॐ श्रीमद्भगवद्गीतासूपनिषत्सु ब्रह्मविद्यायां योगशास्त्रे श्रीकृष्णार्जुनसंवादे
om śrīmadbhagavadgītāsūpaniṣatsu brahmavidyāyāṁ yogaśāstre śrīkṛṣṇārjunasaṁvāde
दैवासुरसम्पद्विभागयोगो नाम षोडशोऽध्यायः श्लोकः ४
daivāsurasampadvibhāgayogo nāma ṣoḍaśo'dhyāyaḥ ślokaḥ 4

— ॐ —

दम्भो दर्पोऽभिमानश्च क्रोधः पारुष्यमेव च ।
dambho darpo'bhimānaśca krodhaḥ pāruṣyameva ca
अज्ञानं चाभिजातस्य पार्थ सम्पदमासुरीम् ॥१६-४॥
ajñānaṁ cābhijātasya pārtha sampadamāsurīm (16-4)

Ostentation, arrogance, self-conceit, anger, rudeness, ignorance—these are the marks of one born with Demoniac affluence. (16.4)

—: Word-by-Word :—

दम्भः dambhaḥ – hypocrisy; दर्पः darpaḥ – arrogance; अभिमानः abhimānaḥ – pride; च ca – and; क्रोधः krodhaḥ – anger; पारुष्यम् pāruṣyam – harshness; एव ca – as well as; अज्ञानम् ajñānam – ignorance; च ca – and; अभिजातस्य abhijātasya – born of; पार्थ pārtha – O son of Prithā; सम्पदम् sampadam – the qualities; आसुरीम् āsurīm – demoniac.

—: Understanding The Verse :—

— ॐ श्रीकृष्णाय नमः ॐ —

Having unveiled the serene and elevating qualities of the दैवी सम्पदा daivī-sampadā—the virtues worthy of reverence and cultivation—Shri Bhagwāna now turns His compassionate yet unsparing gaze upon the stark opposite side.

In this verse we step into the shadowed terrain where the Lord outlines the आसुरी सम्पदा āsurī-sampadā, the demoniac endowments that bind the soul in deeper layers of saṁsāric bondage.

Here, the spiritual light recedes momentarily, revealing the darkened currents of human nature—those qualities born of tamas and rajas, steeped in ignorance and driven by the ego's insatiable hunger.

— ॐ श्रीरामाय नमः ॐ —

Oh, how the verse turns dark: to the qualities belonging to those born with demoniac endowments (āsurī-sampadāḥ). In this verse, six such traits are enumerated: (1) ostentation or hypocrisy (दम्भः dambhaḥ); (2) arrogance (दर्पः darpaḥ); (3) self-conceit or egoism

(अभिमानः abhimānaḥ); (4) anger (क्रोधः krodhaḥ); (5) harshness or rudeness (पारुष्यं pāruṣyam); and (6) ignorance (अज्ञानम् ajñānam). These six are the natural marks of those of demoniac nature, inclining them toward delusion, bondage, and downfall.

— ॐ काकभुशुण्डिसंसेव्याय नमः ॐ —

Where verses 16.1–3 sang of luminosity, purity, and inward peace, verse 16.4 reveals traits forged in the crucible of delusion and misidentification.

Hypocrisy, arrogance, pride, wrath, harshness, ignorance are enumerated as the hallmarks of āsuric temperament. Each of these is not just a moral failing but a symptom of deeper spiritual blindness—a state in which the jīva, estranged from its true Self, becomes ensnared in the fleeting pleasures and pains of the world.

— ॐ अच्युताय नमः ॐ —

These qualities, though common in the human condition, are corrosive both to the individual soul and to the wider fabric of society. They foster inner unrest and external discord, obstructing the path to self-knowledge and impeding the blossoming of higher awareness—the knowledge of who-I-am.

Thus, this verse serves both as a warning and a mirror, urging us to discern and renounce these detrimental tendencies, lest they crystallize into a destiny far removed from the Divine—which is our innate nature except for the murk of debris and dirt that has become crusted upon us over many a lifetime.

—: Key Sanskrit Terms :—

— ॐ तत सत ॐ —

Lo, here we hear the Sanskrit as alike a thunder rolling heavy. Hypocrisy, arrogance, anger, harshness—each word like a dark cloud gathering weight. O mortal, let us never become weighed down with these—and it is for this reason that Bhagwāna Shri Krishna delineates them here.

Now let us loosen the verse's folds, not tearing but touching—allowing the Sanskrit terms to breathe, to stir, to remind, to caution.

— ॐ —

दम्भः (Dambhaḥ) – Ostentation / Hypocrisy:
दम्भ Dambha is the outward show of virtue without its inner substance. It is spiritual pretense, a false projection of piety or wisdom.

The दम्भि dambhī seeks praise, not truth; recognition, not realization.

— ॐ —

दर्पः (Darpaḥ) – Arrogance / Insolence:
Rooted in pride of strength, wealth, or knowledge, दर्प darpa is the haughtiness that sees others as lesser. It blinds the intellect बुद्धि (buddhi), making humility impossible and consequently Self-knowledge unattainable.

— ॐ —

अभिमानः (Abhimānaḥ) – Egotism / Self-conceit:
From the root मान "man" (to think), अभिमान abhimāna is the deep-seated identification with the ego—the "I am this body, I am this mind, I am this role; I am such and so."
It is the primary veil of माया māyā, the illusion of separateness and doership.

— ॐ —

क्रोधः (Krodhaḥ) – Anger:
Born of obstructed desire, क्रोध krodha is the fire that consumes discernment.
As also stated in Gītā 2.63: क्रोधाद्भवति सम्मोहः *krodhāt bhavati sammohah*—from anger arises delusion.
It is the sign of a disturbed, ungoverned mind.

— ॐ —

पारुष्यं (Pāruṣyam) – Harshness / Rudeness:
Speech or behavior devoid of दया dayā and मार्दव mārdava—the very opposite in fact.
पारुष्यं Pāruṣyam wounds not only others, but the very संस्कार samskāras of the speaker, coarsening the soul and estranging it further from our Source: Braham, who is सत्यम् शिवम् सुन्दरम् satyaṁ-śivam-sundaram.

— ॐ —

अज्ञानम् (Ajñānam) – Ignorance / Spiritual blindness:
This is not lack of information, but the अविद्या avidyā which is veiling the Self.
अज्ञान Ajñāna is mistaking the impermanent for the permanent, the body for the Self, the world for the Real.
It is the very womb of all the other āsuric traits.

— ॐ —

अभिजातस्य (Abhijātasya) – Born into / inclined toward:

Just as in 16.3, here it denotes one whose inner disposition (due to past karma and vāsanās) inclines them toward these āsuric tendencies. Such a person is not condemned, but veiled—misdirected in their search for fulfillment.

— ॐ —

पार्थ (Pārtha) – O son of Pṛthā (Arjuna):

The address is intimate and instructive. By calling him Pārtha, Shri Krishna reminds Arjuna of his noble heritage—a subtle urging to renounce these lower impulses and rise to the दैवी सम्पदा daivī sampadā.

Let the Pārtha in thee awaken too, O mortal, O modern day Arjuna!

— ॐ —

संपदम् आसुरीम् (Sampadam Āsurīm) – Demoniacal endowment:

Āsura does not merely mean "demonic" in mythological terms, but refers to a state of being consumed by duality, desire, and darkness.

It is the inner empire of the ego, where Truth is veiled and the Divine forgotten.

—: In Brief :—

— ॐ श्रीकृष्णाय नमः ॐ —

In this sobering verse, Shri Krishna lays bare the marks of the आसुरी āsuric nature—a temperament entangled in sense pleasures and bereft of the vision of higher truth.

The term आसुर 'Asura' signifies not some mythic demon but any person whose mind is engrossed in worldly pursuits, who has forsaken the goal of God-realization for transient enjoyments.

Such a being, guided by false knowledge and unchecked desire, accumulates demoniac traits as naturally as a tree draws sustenance from its roots.

— ॐ कोसलाधीशाय नमः ॐ —

Particularly noteworthy is the mention of अज्ञान ajñāna, or ignorance—not merely ignorance of worldly facts, but the profound absence of discernment between the real and the unreal, between virtue and vice, between dharma and adharma.

This ignorance serves as the fertile ground from which all other negative traits sprout.

When a person mistakes the ephemeral for the eternal and clings to egoic illusions, the āsuric properties manifest effortlessly—and hypocrisy now festers; and pride swells; and anger flares; and cruelty becomes commonplace. Such a path leads inevitably to moral decay and spiritual ruin.

— ॐ श्रीरामाय नमः ॐ —

Having now described the distinct characteristics of both the divine and the demoniac dispositions, Bhagwāna next prepares to reveal the fruits of these two divergent paths. In the next verse He speaks of the ultimate destiny that awaits those who cultivate either set of qualities—thus offering both a stern reminder and a message of hope.

Importantly, Shri Krishna reassures Arjuna—whose heart may tremble upon hearing of the demoniac traits—that he is indeed born with the divine nature, thus rekindling courage and resolve in the midst of this weighty discourse.

— ॐ तत सत ॐ —

Before we move on, let us bow in reverence to this sacred verse—a timeless beacon of wisdom guiding seekers for ages. Write it by hand, reflect on its meaning, and chant it aloud, for these sounds alone carry the authenticity of that era. The world may have changed but the living vibration of these Sanskrit sounds still remain as original as they were when Bhagwān Shri Krishna Himself walked the earth and imparted these teachings.

— ॐ —

दम्भो दर्पोऽभिमानश्च क्रोधः पारुष्यमेव च ।
dambho darpo'bhimānaśca krodhaḥ pāruṣyameva ca
अज्ञानं चाभिजातस्य पार्थ सम्पदमासुरीम् ॥ १६-४ ॥
ajñānaṁ cābhijātasya pārtha sampadamāsurīm (16-4)

— ॐ —

दम्भो दर्पोऽभिमानश्च क्रोधः पारुष्यमेव च ।
dambho darpo'bhimānaśca krodhaḥ pāruṣyameva ca
अज्ञानं चाभिजातस्य पार्थ सम्पदमासुरीम् ॥ १६-४ ॥
ajñānaṁ cābhijātasya pārtha sampadamāsurīm (16-4)

ॐ तत्सदिति श्रीमद्भगवद्गीतासूपनिषत्सु ब्रह्मविद्यायां योगशास्त्रे श्रीकृष्णार्जुनसंवादे
om tatsaditi śrīmadbhagavadgītāsūpaniṣatsu brahmavidyāyāṁ yogaśāstre śrīkṛṣṇārjunasaṁvāde
दैवासुरसम्पद्विभागयोगो नाम षोडशोऽध्यायः श्लोकः ४
daivāsurasampadvibhāgayogo nāma ṣoḍaśo'dhyāyaḥ ślokaḥ 4

Om-Tat-Sat—Om (Braham) is the sole Reality. In the Yogic Scripture on the Science-of-Braham, the Shrimada-Bhāgvada-Gītā Upanishad, we hereby conclude Shloka 4 of the Dialogue between Shrī Krishna and Arjuna entitled Daivāsura-Sampada-Vibhāga-Yoga, Canto XVI.

ॐ गीता श्लोकः १६.५ – GĪTĀ VERSE 16.5

ॐ श्रीमद्भगवद्गीतासूपनिषत्सु ब्रह्मविद्यायां योगशास्त्रे श्रीकृष्णार्जुनसंवादे
om śrīmadbhagavadgītāsūpaniṣatsu brahmavidyāyāṁ yogaśāstre śrīkṛṣṇārjunasaṁvāde
दैवासुरसम्पद्विभागयोगो नाम षोडशोऽध्यायः श्लोकः ५
daivāsurasampadvibhāgayogo nāma ṣoḍaśo'dhyāyaḥ ślokaḥ 5

— ॐ —

दैवी सम्पद्विमोक्षाय निबन्धायासुरी मता ।
daivī sampadvimokṣāya nibandhāyāsurī matā
मा शुचः सम्पदं दैवीमभिजातोऽसि पाण्डव ॥१६-५॥
mā śucaḥ sampadaṁ daivīmabhijāto'si pāṇḍava (16-5)

Divine endowment has been recognized as conducive to liberation, and the demoniac as leading to bondage. Grieve not, O Pāndava, for you are born with divine propensities. (16.5)

—: Word-by-Word :—

दैवी daivī – divine qualities; **सम्पत्** sampat – lead to liberation; **विमोक्षाय** vimokṣāya – freedom; **निबन्धाय** nibandhāya – lead to bondage; **आसुरी** āsurī – demoniac qualities; **मता** matā – are considered; **मा** śucaḥ – do not grieve; **सम्पदम्** sampadam – the qualities; **दैवीम्** daivīm – divine; **अभिजातः** abhijātaḥ – born of; **असि** asi – you are; **पाण्डव** pāṇḍava – O son of Pāṇḍu.

—: Understanding The Verse :—

— ॐ श्रीकृष्णाय नमः ॐ —

We now arrive at Bhagavad-Gītā 16.5—a verse that stands like the tender light of dawn after a night of stark contrasts. Having delineated the luminous path of divine virtues and the shadowed course of demoniac traits, Shri Bhagwāna now draws a clear and decisive line between their ultimate fruits: liberation for those adorned with **दैवी सम्पदा** daivī-sampadā and bondage for those ensnared by the **आसुरी सम्पदा** āsurī-sampadā.

Shri Krishna crisply sums up the distinction here: "The divine endowment leads to liberation, while the demoniac endowment leads to bondage; therefore you O Pārtha—who are born with the divine nature—should take refuge in those qualities that uplift and emancipate, avoiding those that bind and destroy."

Even as He lays bare this truth with precision, the Lord's voice softens, offering reassurance and solace to Arjuna—His beloved disciple and friend—affirming that he is indeed born with the divine propensities.

— ॐ श्रीरामाय नमः ॐ —

This verse is both a summary and a turning point, contrasting the divergent ends of spiritual evolution. The दैवी daivī nature—composed of sattvic virtues such as purity, humility, patience, and compassion—naturally leads one to मोक्ष mokṣa, the ultimate freedom that unites the soul with Braham, the Supreme.

In contrast, the आसुरी āsuric nature—rooted in arrogance, deceit, cruelty, and ignorance—draws the jīva deeper into संसार saṁsāra, the cyclical bondage of birth and death.

— ॐ सत्यवाचे नमः ॐ —

Yet more than a mere philosophical statement, this verse serves as a spiritual beacon. It illumines the transformative power of divine qualities, showing how their cultivation gradually dissolves the knots of material attachment and harmonizes the individual with the will of the Supreme.

Conversely, it warns of the peril of unchecked egoism and worldliness, which, like dark vines, entangle and pull the soul away from his true destiny.

The Lord's tender assurance to Arjuna underscores a profound Vedantic truth: that the divine nature, once awakened, assures the aspirant's ultimate liberation.

Thus, the verse weaves together the inexorable law of karma and the emancipating grace of Sanātana-Dharma—affirming that the path of virtue is the path of true freedom.

—: *Key Sanskrit Terms* :—

— ॐ तत सत ॐ —

Now let us follow the winding path of the verse's language as one might follow a stream into forest depth—trusting the Sanskrit flow to lead us somewhere still, somewhere very ancient.

The Sanskrit stream here seems to split in two, suggestive of the two kinds in the world: daivas and āsuras.

Let us make sure we are flowing in the right stream.

And for us to know what is what, each word of the verse appears to divide with a clarity sharp and final—like a mirror cracked; so that knowing of the scissures of human nature, we ourselves stay un-cracked.

— ॐ —

दैवी सम्पत् (Daivī Sampad) – Divine endowment:

Already expounded in verses 16.1–3, this term encapsulates qualities that reflect purity, humility, clarity, restraint, and Self-knowledge. It is the wealth सम्पत् (sampad) of those aligned with dharma and the inward path.

— ॐ —

विमोक्षाय (Vimokṣāya) – For liberation:

Derived from the root मुच muc (to release), विमोक्ष vimokṣa is final liberation—the dissolution of individuality in the Infinite.

The दैवी daivī nature leads to मोक्ष mokṣa by preparing the heart for jñāna and aligning the will with satya (Truth).

— ॐ —

निबन्धाय (Nibandhāya) – For bondage:

निबन्ध Nibandha means tie, attachment, or fetter.

The आसुरी सम्पद āsurī-sampad, characterized by pride, anger, ignorance, and delusion, leads to further entanglement in saṁsāra—the cycle of birth and death governed by karma.

— ॐ —

आसुरी (Āsurī) – Demoniacal:

As clarified before, this term signifies not external evil but the inner state veiled by अहंकार ego and अविद्या avidyā.

The āsura is one who has turned away from the Self, seeking fulfillment through the impermanent.

— ॐ रघुपतये नमः ॐ —

मा शुचः (Mā śucah) – Grieve not / Do not sorrow:

An endearing admonition. मा Mā is a gentle negation, शुचः śucah means grief.

This phrase echoes through the Gītā, where Krishna time and again urges Arjuna to cast off sorrow born of ignorance. It is both a comfort and a command.

— ॐ —

सम्पदं दैवीम् अभिजातः (Sampadaṁ Daivīm Abhijātaḥ) – Born with divine qualities:

अभिजातः Abhijātaḥ implies innate disposition.

Arjuna is recognized as दिव्य संस्कारवान divya-saṁskāravān—one whose inner nature, shaped by past lives of righteousness and spiritual pursuit, is already inclined toward the Divine.

— ॐ —

पाण्डव (Pāṇḍava) – Son of Pāṇḍu (Arjuna):

The invocation of lineage here is not casual. It evokes ancestral dharma, reminding Arjuna that he is heir to a noble stream of सत्य satya, शौर्य śaurya, and धर्म निष्ठ dharma-niṣṭhā.

This lineage, symbolic of inner strength and righteousness, affirms Arjuna's innate suitability for the path of jñāna.

—: In Brief :—

— ॐ श्रीकृष्णाय नमः ॐ —

This verse encapsulates a profound doctrine: that **the divine treasure**— consisting of the sattvic virtues and dharmic practices expounded in verses 1 to 3—**secure our emancipation**: which is freedom from the entanglements of material existence and eventually **gaining our oneness with the Supreme-Absolute**, who is Sat-Cit-Ānanda Braham: the ocean of existence-bliss-consciousness, and **whose manifest form is Bhagwāna Shri Krishna**.

This is no mere theory but is **borne out** by the unbroken **testimony** of the Vedas, the Smṛtis, and the **lived realization** of sages who have walked the path and **arrived** at its glorious summit.

Thus, when the Lord declares that the divine nature is conducive to liberation, He affirms an eternal truth: that **Dharmic living—following the way of Sanātana-Dharma—is the bridge to mokṣa**.

Conversely, the demoniac nature—briefly characterized in verse 16.4 as steeped in tamas and propelled by rajasic agitation—leads inexorably to bondage. Its fruits are restlessness, suffering, and spiritual downfall.

Those who cultivate such traits become enmeshed in worldly trammels, their vision obscured, their lives driven by ephemeral desires.

Here too, the authority of śāstra and the wisdom of saints bear witness: Adharma inevitably reaps the bitter harvest of bondage and sorrows.

— ॐ श्रीरामाय नमः ॐ —

The latter part of this verse is a balm to the anxious heart.

Lest Arjuna—or any earnest seeker who walks the way of Gītā-Yoga—become disheartened by the stern dichotomy, Shri Krishna dispels all doubt with His gracious reassurance: "Grieve not, O Pāṇḍava, for you are born with divine endowments"—ye who follow the path of Sanātana-Dharma. The very fact that you get to read the Gītā—says it clear: Thou art a fortunate soul!

In this single utterance, the Lord acknowledges Arjuna's inherent spiritual nobility and, by extension, offers hope to all aspirants of Daivi propensities, who strive sincerely to live by Sanātana-Dharma.

No matter how daunting the path may appear at first, those anchored in divine qualities are assured of union with the Divine—this is the promise of Bhagwāna Shri Krishna in the Bhagavad-Gītā.

— ॐ मायामानुष चरित्राय नमः ॐ —

As we now move forward, the Lord, having briefly introduced the āsuric nature, prepares to expand upon it in detail. Shri Krishna will examine the inner fabric and outward behaviors of those who embody demoniac tendencies, so that we seekers can become equipped with discerning vision—to recognize and renounce the dark tendencies that obstruct the soul's ascent.

Thusly, the sacred dialogue of the Gītā deepens as we proceed verse by verse, step by step—offering both diagnosis and remedy for the human condition.

— ॐ तत सत ॐ —

Before we move on, let us bow in reverence to this sacred verse—a timeless beacon of wisdom guiding seekers for ages. Write it by hand, reflect on its meaning, and chant it aloud, for these sounds alone carry the authenticity of that era. The world may have changed but the living vibration of these Sanskrit sounds still remain as original as they were when Bhagwān Shri Krishna Himself walked the earth and imparted these teachings.

— ॐ —

दैवी सम्पद्विमोक्षाय निबन्धायासुरी मता ।
daivī sampadvimokṣāya nibandhāyāsurī matā
मा शुचः सम्पदं दैवीमभिजातोऽसि पाण्डव ॥१६-५॥
mā śucaḥ sampadaṁ daivīmabhijāto'si pāṇḍava (16-5)

—ॐ—

दैवी सम्पद्विमोक्षाय निबन्धायासुरी मता ।
daivī sampadvimokṣāya nibandhāyāsurī matā
मा शुचः सम्पदं दैवीमभिजातोऽसि पाण्डव ॥१६-५॥
mā śucaḥ sampadaṁ daivīmabhijāto'si pāṇḍava (16-5)

ॐ तत्सदिति श्रीमद्भगवद्गीतासूपनिषत्सु ब्रह्मविद्यायां योगशास्त्रे श्रीकृष्णार्जुनसंवादे
om tatsaditi śrīmadbhagavadgītāsūpaniṣatsu brahmavidyāyāṁ yogaśāstre śrīkṛṣṇārjunasaṁvāde
दैवासुरसम्पद्विभागयोगो नाम षोडशोऽध्यायः श्लोकः ५
daivāsurasampadvibhāgayogo nāma ṣoḍaśo'dhyāyaḥ ślokaḥ 5

Om-Tat-Sat—Om (Braham) is the sole Reality. In the Yogic Scripture on the Science-of-Braham, the Shrimada-Bhāgvada-Gītā Upanishad, we hereby conclude Shloka 5 of the Dialogue between Shrī Krishna and Arjuna entitled Daivāsura-Sampada-Vibhāga-Yoga, Canto XVI.

ॐ गीता श्लोकः १६.६ – GĪTĀ VERSE 16.6

ॐ श्रीमद्भगवद्गीतासूपनिषत्सु ब्रह्मविद्यायां योगशास्त्रे श्रीकृष्णार्जुनसंवादे
om śrīmadbhagavadgītāsūpaniṣatsu brahmavidyāyāṁ yogaśāstre śrīkṛṣṇārjunasaṁvāde
दैवासुरसम्पद्विभागयोगो नाम षोडशोऽध्यायः श्लोकः ६
daivāsurasampadvibhāgayogo nāma ṣoḍaśo'dhyāyaḥ ślokaḥ 6

— ॐ —

द्वौ भूतसर्गौ लोकेऽस्मिन्दैव आसुर एव च ।
dvau bhūtasargau loke'smindaiva āsura eva ca
दैवो विस्तरशः प्रोक्त आसुरं पार्थ मे श्रृणु ॥ १६-६ ॥
daivo vistaraśaḥ prokta āsuraṁ pārtha me śṛṇu (16-6)

Of beings, there are two types—the Divine and the Demoniacal. The Divine kind has been described at length; now hear from me of the Demoniacal type, O Pārtha. (16.6)

—: Word-by-Word :—

द्वौ dvau – two; भूतसर्गौ bhūtasargau – types of beings; लोके loke – in this world; अस्मिन् asmin – in this; दैव daivaḥ – the divine; आसुरः āsuraḥ – the demoniac; एव ca – and; दैवः daivaḥ – the divine; विस्तरशः vistaraśaḥ – at length; प्रोक्तः proktaḥ – has been described; आसुरम् āsuram – the demoniac; पार्थ pārtha – O son of Prithā; मे me – by me; श्रृणु śṛṇu – hear.

—: Understanding The Verse :—

— ॐ श्रीकृष्णाय नमः ॐ —

With śloka 16.6 we now stand at a pivotal threshold in Bhagavad-Gītā—a verse that acts as a bridge between two turgid streams of human disposition. Here, Shri Bhagwāna, with both clarity and compassion, shifts focus from the दैवी सम्पदा daivī-sampadā—the divine nature extolled in earlier verses—to the आसुरी सम्पदा āsurī bhāva, the demoniac temperament that ensnares the soul in the endless wheel of saṁsāra.

Mind it, this is not merely a theoretical classification but a deep insight into the inner architecture of the human condition, revealing the subtle currents that shape one's destiny.

— ॐ श्रीरामाय नमः ॐ —

Lord Krishna proclaims the essential polarity that runs through all beings: the divine and the demoniac. While both tendencies may arise within the human heart, their direction and ultimate end are starkly different.

The divine nature aligns itself with dharma, seeking unity with the Supreme and liberation from material bondage; the demoniac nature, by contrast, turns away from the light, rooting itself in ego, desire, and delusion, which tighten the chains of worldly entrapments.

— ॐ ऋष्यशृंगपूजिताय नमः ॐ —

Shri Bhagwāna reminds Arjuna that the divine nature has already been described earlier by Him—providing both a blueprint for spiritual ascent and a mirror for honest self-assessment. Now, Shri Krishna urges Arjuna to pay attention as He reveals the characteristics of the demoniac nature.

Why turn to examine the darker side of human disposition?
Because awareness is protection.
By understanding these tendencies, one learns to recognize their presence within and around, and to guard against their subtle pull.

Thus, this verse functions as a cautionary teaching and, at the same time, as a profound invitation to self-awareness.

Each of us is called to discern these two dispositions within us—and to consciously renounce the lower, and to rise steadfastly toward the light of the divine.

—: *Key Sanskrit Terms* :—

— ॐ तत सत ॐ —

Now let us listen for the pulse of meaning beneath the verse's surface—where the Sanskrit terms beat softly like a hidden drum sounding warnings while also calling us inward.

— ॐ —

द्वौ (Dvau) – Two:
This term opens the verse with distinction—indicating that there are two fundamental types or paths of beings **भूतसर्गौ** (bhūtasargau).
In the non-dual philosophy of Vedānta, such divisions are provisional, intended for instruction, and are eventually transcended in the realization of Oneness.

— ॐ —

भूतसर्गौ (Bhūta-sargau) – Creations or Categories of Beings:
From **भूत** bhūta (being, entity) and **सर्ग** sarga (creation, category), this compound suggests two primary ontological orientations in which beings manifest and evolve.

These are not classifications by castes, species, or rigid classes, but states of spiritual consciousness.

— ॐ —

लोकेऽस्मिन् (Loke'smin) – In this world:

This reinforces the immediacy and universality of the teaching—it is not abstract or mythological, but applicable here, now, in this realm अस्मिन् लोके (asmin loke), where all action unfolds.

— ॐ —

दैवः (Daivaḥ) – The Divine type:

Already elaborated in verses 16.1–3, the दैव daiva disposition reflects sāttvic qualities—purity, truth, humility, devotion, and Self-knowledge; it leads one toward liberation मोक्ष (mokṣa)—union with the Divine.

— ॐ —

आसुरः (Āsuraḥ) – The Demoniacal type:

The āsura nature—briefly described in 16.4 and to be described now in more detail—is not physical (of hideaous monstrous beings) but of inner spiritual ignorance—dominated by rājas (passion) and tamas (inertia).

It is marked by ego, desire, delusion, and an insurrection against Dharma.

— ॐ —

विस्तरशः (Vistaraśaḥ) – In detail / at length:

Indicates that the daivī nature has already been explained fully and with care—suggesting its primacy and desirability in the spiritual life.

— ॐ —

प्रोक्त (Prokta) – Has been spoken:

A gentle reminder that the instruction is already imparted, preparing the listener to now contrast and deeply understand the opposite disposition.

— ॐ —

पार्थ (Pārtha) – O son of Pṛthā (Arjuna):

A name laden with spiritual intimacy and ancestral dharma.

It again affirms Arjuna's—and of all souls walking the path of Gītā-Dharma—innate nobility drawing him away from despair or doubt, and preparing him to hear without fear or judgment.

— ॐ —

मे शृणु (Me Śṛṇu) – Hear from Me; listen to me:

Of course Krishna knows Arjuna is attentively listening, but this word is an affectionate imperative—which one uses when imparting something of import to someone close.

शृणु Śṛṇu (hear) implies more than auditory reception—it is a call to receptive listening, a sacred readiness to absorb शब्द ब्रह्म śabda-brahman (Divine Word)—and in this case it is directly from the very lips of Lord-God Bhagwāna Shri Krishna Himself – who is the very manifest form of satt-chitt-ānanda Braham, the Creator, our Maker.

—: In Brief :—

— ॐ श्रीकृष्णाय नमः ॐ —

In this verse, Shri Bhagwāna declares the fundamental bifurcation of beings into two broad categories: the divine and the demoniac.

This is not to suggest an absolute division but rather to highlight the twin currents flowing through creation—one that elevates and liberates, and another that binds and degrades;

and which make this crazy show possible—this sport of Braham, this Līlā of Shri Krishna.

Each being, composed of both sentient spirit and insentient matter, manifests qualities that arise from their orientation:

- When the conscious self inclines toward prakṛti, or material nature, demoniac tendencies are stirred;
- When it yearns for the Lord, for the Self, for realizing who-I-am, the divine nature awakens.

And of course this quest is circular—one feeding the other.

— ॐ श्रीरामाय नमः ॐ —

The word दैव 'Deva' signifies the radiant, the godly—that which aspires upward, seeking the imperishable. Hence, all means that lead to God-realization—truth, compassion, humility, purity—are recognized as expressions of the divine nature.

Conversely, when one identifies with the insentient and transitory, turning away from the Supreme, the darker traits of egoism, arrogance, and cruelty take root.

Mind it, it is the human being, endowed with viveka (discrimination), who is shown standing here at the crossroads of these paths. Unlike other beings—whether gods, suras, asuras, nagas, daityas, devas, gandharvas, rakshasas, beasts, spirits—man holds the unique power to renounce the demoniac and, through steadfast effort and grace, allow the divine nature to shine forth.

— ॐ सुन्दराय नमः ॐ —

Thus, Shri Krishna not only frames the contrast but sets the stage for deeper exploration.

Inviting Arjuna—and by extension all us seekers—to lend ear and heart, Krishna next prepares to describe, with penetrating detail, the characteristics and conduct of those possessed by the demoniac nature

—so that we become aware of the treacherous path that lead straight to hell

—for us to stay alert, so that we ourselves do not become them.

In the verses that follow, the Lord will illuminate these tendencies fully, empowering the aspirant with the wisdom to recognize, reject, and rise beyond them.

— ॐ तत सत ॐ —

Before moving on, let us once more bow in deep reverence before this sacred verse of the Bhagavad-Gītā, an eternal beacon of wisdom that ceaselessly illumines the path of seekers. Engage with its form—inscribe it with your own hand, let your heart dwell upon its meaning, and raise your voice in its chanting—for within these syllables echoes the undying proclamation delivered millennia ago on the battlefield of Kurukshetra. These words, transmitted unchanged across the unbroken chain of generations, form a living bridge, linking us to that sanctified era when Bhagwāna Shri Krishna Himself walked this earth and bestowed this divine teaching. Through the luminous vibration of these sacred Sanskrit sounds, we are drawn nearer to His timeless presence, touching the very heartbeat of the Eternal.

— ॐ —

द्वौ भूतसर्गौ लोकेऽस्मिन्दैव आसुर एव च ।
dvau bhūtasargau loke'smindaiva āsura eva ca
दैवो विस्तरशः प्रोक्त आसुरं पार्थ मे शृणु ॥ १६-६ ॥
daivo vistaraśaḥ prokta āsuraṁ pārtha me śṛṇu (16-6)

— ॐ —

द्वौ भूतसर्गौ लोकेऽस्मिन्दैव आसुर एव च ।
dvau bhūtasargau loke'smindaiva āsura eva ca
दैवो विस्तरशः प्रोक्त आसुरं पार्थ मे शृणु ॥ १६-६ ॥
daivo vistaraśaḥ prokta āsuraṁ pārtha me śṛṇu (16-6)

ॐ तत्सदिति श्रीमद्भगवद्गीतासूपनिषत्सु ब्रह्मविद्यायां योगशास्त्रे श्रीकृष्णार्जुनसंवादे
om tatsaditi śrīmadbhagavadgītāsūpaniṣatsu brahmavidyāyāṁ yogaśāstre śrīkṛṣṇārjunasaṁvāde
दैवासुरसम्पद्विभागयोगो नाम षोडशोऽध्यायः श्लोकः ६
daivāsurasampadvibhāgayogo nāma ṣoḍaśo'dhyāyaḥ ślokaḥ 6

Om-Tat-Sat—Om (Braham) is the sole Reality. In the Yogic Scripture on the Science-of-Braham, the Shrimada-Bhāgvada-Gītā Upanishad, we hereby conclude Shloka 6 of the Dialogue between Shrī Krishna and Arjuna entitled Daivāsura-Sampada-Vibhāga-Yoga, Canto XVI.

ॐ गीता श्लोकः १६.७ – GĪTĀ VERSE 16.7

ॐ श्रीमद्भगवद्गीतासूपनिषत्सु ब्रह्मविद्यायां योगशास्त्रे श्रीकृष्णार्जुनसंवादे
om śrīmadbhagavadgītāsūpaniṣatsu brahmavidyāyāṁ yogaśāstre śrīkṛṣṇārjunasaṁvāde
दैवासुरसम्पद्विभागयोगो नाम षोडशोऽध्यायः श्लोकः ७
daivāsurasampadvibhāgayogo nāma ṣoḍaśo'dhyāyaḥ ślokaḥ 7

— ॐ —

प्रवृत्तिं च निवृत्तिं च जना न विदुरासुराः ।
pravṛttiṁ ca nivṛttiṁ ca janā na vidurāsurāḥ
न शौचं नापि चाचारो न सत्यं तेषु विद्यते ॥१६-७॥
na śaucaṁ nāpi cācāro na satyaṁ teṣu vidyate (16-7)

Those of demoniac disposition—they are unconcerned as to what are prescribed works or prohibited acts; they have neither purity, nor proper conduct, nor truthfulness. (16.7)

—: Word-by-Word :—

प्रवृत्तिम् pravṛttim – proper action; **च** ca – and; **निवृत्तिम्** nivṛttim – proper abstention; **च** ca – and; **जनाः** janāḥ – people; **न** na – not; **विदुः** viduḥ – know; **आसुराः** āsurāḥ – those of demoniac nature; **न** na – neither; **शौचम्** śaucam – cleanliness; **नापि** na api – nor; **च** ca – and; **आचारः** ācāraḥ – proper conduct; **न** na – nor; **सत्यम्** satyam – truth; **तेषु** teṣu – in them; **विद्यते** vidyate – exists.

—: Understanding The Verse :—

— ॐ श्रीकृष्णाय नमः ॐ —

We now descend further into the shadowed recesses of human nature as Shri Bhagwāna, with unflinching precision, illumines the dark **आसुरी भाव** āsurī bhāva in verse 16.7.

This verse penetrates beyond superficial conduct to expose a deeper spiritual malaise: the inner disorder that arises when discernment is lost, when the guiding light of dharma is obscured, and when man wanders, untethered, through the forest of saṁsāra.

The āsuric nature is unveiled here not as mere external behavior but as an existential condition—where the moral compass is shattered, the intellect is muddied by ignorance, and the heart stands estranged from purity and truth.

— ॐ श्रीरामाय नमः ॐ —

Shri Krishna describes those of demoniac disposition as utterly bereft of viveka—the power to discern what is to be undertaken **प्रवृत्ति** (pravṛtti) and what is to be renounced **निवृत्ति** (nivṛtti).

In their blindness, such beings fail to recognize the sanctity of scriptural injunctions and the subtle demands of dharma.

Lacking inner and outer purity शौच (śauca), noble conduct आचार (ācāra), and truthfulness सत्य (satya), their lives become arenas of unchecked desire and heedless action. Their allegiance is not to higher ideals but to fleeting gratifications, which only deepen their bondage.

— ॐ अधर्मनाशकाय नमः ॐ —

Do know: This verse is not hurled as an accusation but offered as a mirror—an invitation for the seeker to sharpen his discernment, to recognize these patterns both within and without, and to vigilantly guard the sanctity of his own spiritual path.

It is a solemn reminder that without the anchor of Sanātana-Dharma, life becomes disordered, indulgent, and ultimately self-destructive.

—: Key Sanskrit Terms :—

— ॐ तत सत ॐ —

Now let us hear to the individual sounds of the verse—which here sound like voices lost in wilderness. The demonic know not what to do or refrain from; truth is not in them; and each syllable here reminds us of absence, hollowness, dissonance.

The Sanskrit here isn't there to be held; it's here to slip through the fingers like sand—to feel its texture, like in a prayer to always stay in Dharma and never stray from the path of Gītā-Dharma.

Now let us let go of our needing to 'grasp' everything—and let's just hear the words.

— ॐ —

प्रवृत्तिं (Pravṛttiṁ) – Engagement / Inclined Action:

Derived from the root वृत्त vṛt (to act, to move), with the prefix प्र ra- (forward), प्रवृत्ति pravṛtti refers to the path of engagement in the world—right action (karma), duties, responsibilities, and the external expressions of dharma.

It is the righteous unfolding of life within the framework of cosmic order.

— ॐ —

निवृत्तिं (Nivṛttiṁ) – Withdrawal / Renunciation:

In contrast, निवृत्ति nivṛtti is the path of withdrawal—renunciation, inner detachment, dis-identification from worldly involvement, and movement toward contemplation and Self-realization.

It is the inward return to the-Source.

— ॐ —

जनाः (Janāḥ) – People / Beings:

Here, it refers specifically to those of āsurī nature—embodied souls (jīvās) whose tendencies are clouded by tamas and rājas, veiling clarity and discretion.

— ॐ —

न विदुः (Na viduḥ) – Do not know:

Indicates spiritual ignorance, not merely lack of information. These individuals are cut off from the wisdom that discerns dharma from adharma, right from wrong, real from unreal.

— ॐ —

शौचं (Śaucam) – Purity:

Inner and outer cleanliness—of body, mind, and intention. It is the condition in which truth can take root. Without शौचं śaucam, the heart becomes an unsuitable vessel for higher knowledge. If the vessel is unclean, everything it contains becomes unclean.

— ॐ —

आचारः (Ācāraḥ) – Right conduct / Observance of Dharma:

This is not etiquette, but the lived expression of inner alignment with ऋत ṛta, the cosmic order.

आचार Ācāra links the seen with the unseen, the moral with the metaphysical.

— ॐ —

सत्यं (Satyam) – Truth:

Both verbal truthfulness and alignment with reality सत (sat). It is the expression of what is, unmarred by distortion.

In the आसुरी भाव āsurī bhāva, truth is absent because the ego seeks to preserve its illusions.

— ॐ —

तेषु विद्यते (Teṣu vidyate) – Is not found among them:

This is a firm negation. The verse concludes with a definitive statement: such beings are disconnected from the fundamental principles that sustain dharmic life.

—: *In Brief* :—

— ॐ श्रीकृष्णाय नमः ॐ —

In essence, this verse lays bare a crucial truth: those who possess a demoniac disposition remain ignorant of the distinction between righteous action and its opposite.

They neither comprehend what is to be embraced for spiritual upliftment nor what is to be abandoned as harmful. Thus, their lives are governed not by dharma but by whim, impulse, and the clamor of unrefined desires.

Their failure to recognize the law of right action (karma) and its fruits traps them in a cycle of impurity, misconduct, and falsehood—external and internal disorder reflecting an inner estrangement from truth.

— ॐ श्रीरामाय नमः ॐ —

Shri Bhagwāna emphasizes here that true purity शौच (śauca) encompasses both outer cleanliness and inner sanctity—a state of mind and heart purified of selfish motives and restless passions.

Noble conduct आचार (ācāra) is not merely ritualistic compliance but the living embodiment of ethical and spiritual refinement, while truth सत्य (satya) shines forth as sincerity, integrity, and alignment with reality.

Those of āsuric nature are bereft of these, their existence marked instead by spiritual corrosion.

— ॐ —

Yet the teaching here is deeper still. Beneath the surface of these qualities lies the fundamental Vedantic truth that all dualities—divine and demoniac—arise within the realm of prakṛti, the manifest world.

Beyond this, the Self remains untouched, all-pervading, and indivisible. Though the world appears sustained and shaped by these dual tendencies, ultimately it is only the unworldly, the eternal Braham, that truly is.

As long as this evanescent world appears real to the individual, these dualities must be confronted; but once the veil of māyā lifts, all dissolves back into the singular reality—वसुदेवः सर्वम Vāsudevaḥ sarvam.

— ॐ सुभद्राप्रियाय नमः ॐ —

Having shown the lack of discrimination, purity, and truth in those dominated by demoniac nature, the Lord moves forward. In the next verse He unveils the atheistic and nihilistic outlook that forms the inner creed of such beings, revealing how their distorted understanding further entrenches them in ignorance and suffering.

Blessed we are—the sacred Gītā dialogue continues to play out, peeling back ever deeper layers of the human condition for all earnest seekers to behold.

— ॐ तत सत ॐ —

Before we move on, let us bow in reverence to this sacred verse. Write it by hand, reflect on its meaning, chant it aloud, make it your own.

— ॐ —

प्रवृत्तिं च निवृत्तिं च जना न विदुरासुराः ।
pravṛttiṁ ca nivṛttiṁ ca janā na vidurāsurāḥ
न शौचं नापि चाचारो न सत्यं तेषु विद्यते ॥१६-७॥
na śaucaṁ nāpi cācāro na satyaṁ teṣu vidyate (16-7)

— ॐ —

प्रवृत्तिं च निवृत्तिं च जना न विदुरासुराः ।
pravṛttiṁ ca nivṛttiṁ ca janā na vidurāsurāḥ
न शौचं नापि चाचारो न सत्यं तेषु विद्यते ॥१६-७॥
na śaucaṁ nāpi cācāro na satyaṁ teṣu vidyate (16-7)

ॐ तत्सदिति श्रीमद्भगवद्गीतासूपनिषत्सु ब्रह्मविद्यायां योगशास्त्रे श्रीकृष्णार्जुनसंवादे
om tatsaditi śrīmadbhagavadgītāsūpaniṣatsu brahmavidyāyāṁ yogaśāstre śrīkṛṣṇārjunasaṁvāde
दैवासुरसम्पद्विभागयोगो नाम षोडशोऽध्यायः श्लोकः ७
daivāsurasampadvibhāgayogo nāma ṣoḍaśo'dhyāyaḥ ślokaḥ 7

Om-Tat-Sat—Om (Braham) is the sole Reality. In the Yogic Scripture on the Science-of-Braham, the Shrimada-Bhāgvada-Gītā Upanishad, we hereby conclude Shloka 7 of the Dialogue between Shrī Krishna and Arjuna entitled Daivāsura-Sampada-Vibhāga-Yoga, Canto XVI.

A Broken Compass: Macullû—Macaulay's child.

He walks—but not by the Path,
He speaks and swears—but not by the Truth,
He works—but not by the Prescribed of Sanâtana-Dharma.

No axis, no compass.
Only noise remains in his world—where Dharma once was.

Prescribed Duty and Dharma?
He scoffs at the very word.
Calls it bondage, calls it blind obedience.
He is a man unmoored—and so proud of it !
But his freedom is dissipation, flippancy, emission, discharge —
Far from that powered flight that takes one to the eternal skies.

ॐ गीता श्लोकः १६.८ – GĪTĀ VERSE 16.8

ॐ श्रीमद्भगवद्गीतासूपनिषत्सु ब्रह्मविद्यायां योगशास्त्रे श्रीकृष्णार्जुनसंवादे
om śrīmadbhagavadgītāsūpaniṣatsu brahmavidyāyām̐ yogaśāstre śrīkṛṣṇārjunasam̐vāde
दैवासुरसम्पद्विभागयोगो नाम षोडशोऽध्यायः श्लोकः ८
daivāsurasampadvibhāgayogo nāma ṣoḍaśo'dhyāyaḥ ślokaḥ 8

— ॐ —

असत्यमप्रतिष्ठं ते जगदाहुरनीश्वरम् ।
asatyamapratiṣṭham̐ te jagadāhuranīśvaram
अपरस्परसम्भूतं किमन्यत्कामहैतुकम् ॥१६-८॥
aparasparasambhūtam̐ kimanyatkāmahaitukam (16-8)

They describe the world as without a God, without truth, without foundation, brought forth simply by the union of male and female—as nothing but originating in lust. (16.8)

—: Word-by-Word :—

असत्यम् asatyam – unreal; **अप्रतिष्ठम्** apratiṣṭham – without foundation; **ते** te – they; **जगत्** jagat – the world; **आहुः** āhuḥ – say; **अनीश्वरम्** anīśvaram – without a creator or controller; **अपरस्परसम्भूतम्** aparaspara-sambhūtam – born of mutual union; **किम्** kim – what; **अन्यत्** anyat – else; **कामहैतुकम्** kāma-haitukam – caused by desire.

—: Understanding The Verse :—

— ॐ श्रीकृष्णाय नमः ॐ —

Verse 16.8 is a verse of rare philosophical depth and sobering clarity. In this teaching, Shri Bhagwāna moves from describing mere outward traits of the demoniac nature to unveiling its underlying metaphysical vision—its **दर्शन** darśana, its interpretation of reality.

This is no superficial portrait of immorality, but a penetrating look at the intellectual and existential stance that gives rise to such behavior.

— ॐ श्रीरामाय नमः ॐ —

Here, the Lord lays bare the inner creed of those steeped in **आसुरी भाव** āsurī-bhāva: a worldview devoid of higher truth, stripped of moral foundation, and divorced from any recognition of divine purpose.

For them, the cosmos is a happenstance arising from physical conjunction, a random play of material forces, driven by lust, perpetuated by desires—and ending in nothingness.

Such beings deny not only God ईश्वर (Īśvara) but also Dharma, dismissing the universe as baseless, without origin or higher aim.

Their vision is one of stark materialism—cold, reductionist, and nihilistic.

— ॐ जगद्धिताय कृष्णाय गोविंदाय नमो नमः ॐ —

This verse reveals a profound truth: that a person's actions and character are but the visible outgrowths of their deeper vision of life.

To deny the sacredness of creation, to see existence as a purposeless collision of desires, inevitably leads to moral decay, spiritual blindness, and deeper bondages still.

Shri Krishna, by exposing this worldview, invites us to reflect not merely on outer conduct but on the very lens through which one perceives reality.

This verse serves as both diagnosis and warning—a call to vigilance over the inner convictions—which inner nature alone shapes our destiny.

—: Key Sanskrit Terms :—

— ॐ तत सत ॐ —

The demoniac perceive the world with a smoke screen that blinds the inner eye; they say the world has no foundation; there's no God—it's born of lust and desire alone.

Ah, what a clouded distorted vision these beastly people have!

But let's be warned and make our own vision very clear.

Let us now linger with the verse's innermost Sanskrit expressions — those hallowed sounds in which the breath of the ancient voices still dwells, offering whispers of eternal ancient truths.

— ॐ —

असत्यम् (Asatyam) – Untrue / Denial of truth:

Not merely a lie, but the rejection of ultimate reality **सत** (sat).

In Vedānta, **सत्य** satya is not just factuality, but that which is unchanging, eternal, and real—Braham. The āsuric vision denies this, affirming only the transient, the material.

— ॐ —

अप्रतिष्ठम् (Apratiṣṭham) – Without foundation / rootless:

प्रतिष्ठा Pratiṣṭhā means firm ground, basis, or abiding support.

To deny a foundation is to view existence as accidental, purposeless, adrift—without ऋत ṛta (cosmic order), without dharmic law, without meaning. It is a vision of nihilism.

— ॐ —

ते जगत् आहुः (Te jagad āhuḥ) – They say the world...
ते Te refers to the āsuric ones;
आहुः āhuḥ means "they declare."
This is not accidental ignorance, but a deliberate worldview, the ontological reality for them: their speech reveals the distortions of their inner perception.

— ॐ —

अनिश्वरम् (Anīśvaram) – Without God / without a Lord:
ईश्वर Īśvara is the cosmic intelligence, the inner ruler. To declare the world अनीश्वर an-īśvaram (without that God) is to reject divinity, transcendence, and sacred governance.
It is the heart of materialism—a rampant rebellion against Dharma.

— ॐ —

अपरस्परसम्भूतम् (Aparasparasambhūtam) – Born of mutual union only:
Denotes the belief that the world arises merely from physical processes—the union of opposites, male and female अपरस्परसम्भूतम् aparaspara-sambhūtam – born of mutual union of opposite sex, without any transcendent cause or purpose.
It is a rejection of कारण ब्रहं kāraṇa-brahman, the Divine Cause.

— ॐ —

किमन्यत् (Kim anyat) – What else is there?:
A rhetorical, even sarcastic, dismissal of anything beyond sensual causation.
This reflects existential reductionism—the view that nothing exists beyond matter and instinct!

— ॐ —

काम-हैतुकम् (Kāma-haitukam) – Caused by lust:
The final blow to the sacred. The world, to such thinkers, is not a manifestation of divine will or intelligence, but born of desire काम (kāma)—a product of lust, craving, impulse.
Thus, desire becomes the only deity in this worldview.

—: In Brief :—

— ॐ श्रीकृष्णाय नमः ॐ —

In summary, Shri Bhagwāna vividly portrays the distorted creed of those bound by the demoniac nature: they proclaim that this universe is without root, without inherent truth, and without a governing divinity.

To them, life is but a transient accident, born of the sensual union of male and female, arising from lust and then dissolving into oblivion.

Their worldview denies any higher causality, any divine oversight, and any moral law. For such souls, virtue and vice are illusions, and life's sole aim becomes the satisfaction of carnal desires.

This perspective is not a trivial error but a profound misapprehension of existence, severing the soul from its divine source.

Those who hold such beliefs reject the idea of karma—the law of action and consequence—and scoff at the notion of a supreme Lord who dispenses the fruits of deeds.

In their eyes, those who uphold dharma and reverence the Divine are deluded, clinging to comforting myths. Yet in truth, it is they who are ensnared in avidyā (ignorance), wandering deeper into bondage and suffering.

— ॐ श्रीरामाय नमः ॐ —

With this verse, the Lord unravels the philosophical root of the demoniac temperament, showing how belief—or disbelief—shapes destiny.

Recognizing that such a worldview inevitably breeds moral corruption, Krishna prepares now to illuminate the conduct that naturally springs from it. In the next verses, Shri Bhagwāna anticipates the seeker's unspoken question: "What, then, is the behavior of such unbelievers?"

The teaching will keep unfolding further—revealing the distinctive traits and dangerous paths of those who live by this atheistic outlook.

— ॐ तत सत ॐ —

Before we move on, let us bow in reverence to this sacred verse. Write it by hand, reflect on its meaning, chant it aloud, make it your own.

— ॐ —

असत्यमप्रतिष्ठं ते जगदाहुरनीश्वरम् ।
asatyamapratiṣṭhaṁ te jagadāhuranīśvaram
अपरस्परसम्भूतं किमन्यत्कामहैतुकम् ॥ १६-८ ॥
aparasparasambhūtaṁ kimanyatkāmahaitukam (16-8)

ॐ

असत्यमप्रतिष्ठं ते जगदाहुरनीश्वरम् ।
asatyamapratiṣṭhaṁ te jagadāhuranīśvaram
अपरस्परसम्भूतं किमन्यत्कामहैतुकम् ॥ १६-८ ॥
aparasparasambhūtaṁ kimanyatkāmahaitukam (16-8)

ॐ तत्सदिति श्रीमद्भगवद्गीतासूपनिषत्सु ब्रह्मविद्यायां योगशास्त्रे श्रीकृष्णार्जुनसंवादे
om tatsaditi śrīmadbhagavadgītāsūpaniṣatsu brahmavidyāyāṁ yogaśāstre śrīkṛṣṇārjunasaṁvāde
दैवासुरसम्पद्विभागयोगो नाम षोडशोऽध्यायः श्लोकः ८
daivāsurasampadvibhāgayogo nāma ṣoḍaśo'dhyāyaḥ ślokaḥ 8

Om-Tat-Sat—Om (Braham) is the sole Reality. In the Yogic Scripture on the Science-of-Braham, the Shrimada-Bhāgvada-Gītā Upanishad, we hereby conclude Shloka 8 of the Dialogue between Shrī Krishna and Arjuna entitled Daivāsura-Sampada-Vibhāga-Yoga, Canto XVI.

In the Shrines of Self-Worship.

With God dismissed, man has become his own idol.
He builds altars—not in stone but in self-image.
Man proudly declares: "My 'will' is sacrosanct,"
But others find his 'will' torn in ten thousand directions.
His each desire pulls him thinner, renders him more fragile.

His Child is Raised on Static

The child is told:
There is no design. There is no architect.
Only needs. Only noise. Only physics, chemistry at work.
Man once stared at the stars with wonder.
But today's child can see nothing beyond the Screen's glare.
Sometimes an ancient memory jogs, and he asks: "Who made me?"
He is answered: "Why ask?"

The Lie Seated So Deep

The Ruling-Elites no longer butcher, massacre as they did in past,
Now a day, they do not even wound.
For they found a simpler way: Simply Remove the Holding-Thread,
And the garment of sanity / reality falls apart in Slow Unraveling.

What remains today is a skin-deep civilization,
Pulsing with pleasure, Hollow at the core—
A happy smile painted over vacuousness and chaos.

ॐ गीता श्लोकः १६.९ – GĪTĀ VERSE 16.9

ॐ श्रीमद्भगवद्गीतासूपनिषत्सु ब्रह्मविद्यायां योगशास्त्रे श्रीकृष्णार्जुनसंवादे
om śrīmadbhagavadgītāsūpaniṣatsu brahmavidyāyāṁ yogaśāstre śrīkṛṣṇārjunasaṁvāde
दैवासुरसम्पद्विभागयोगो नाम षोडशोऽध्यायः श्लोकः ९
daivāsurasampadvibhāgayogo nāma ṣoḍaśo'dhyāyaḥ ślokaḥ 9

— ॐ —

एतां दृष्टिमवष्टभ्य नष्टात्मानोऽल्पबुद्धयः ।
etāṁ dṛṣṭimavaṣṭabhya naṣṭātmāno'lpabuddhayaḥ
प्रभवन्त्युग्रकर्माणः क्षयाय जगतोऽहिताः ॥१६-९॥
prabhavantyugrakarmāṇaḥ kṣayāya jagato'hitāḥ (16-9)

Clinging to this false view, these slow-witted men of vile disposition and terrible deeds are born only as enemies of mankind—only for the purpose of destruction of the world. (16.9)

—: Word-by-Word :—

एताम् etām – this; **दृष्टिम्** dṛṣṭim – view; **अवष्टभ्य** avaṣṭabhya – holding firmly; **नष्टात्मानः** naṣṭātmānaḥ – those whose selves are lost; **अल्पबुद्धयः** alpa-buddhayaḥ – of small intelligence; **प्रभवन्ति** prabhavanti – engage; **उग्रकर्माणः** ugra-karmāṇaḥ – in cruel deeds; **क्षयाय** kṣayāya – for the destruction; **जगतः** jagataḥ – of the world; **अहिताः** ahitāḥ – inimical.

—: Understanding The Verse :—

— ॐ श्रीकृष्णाय नमः ॐ —

We now enter the somber precincts of Bhagavad-Gītā 16.9, where the Lord delineates the inevitable descent of those steeped in āsuric tendencies. The verse strikes a solemn chord, weaving together the metaphysical roots and the worldly manifestations of a corrupt inner vision.

Shri Krishna, having previously exposed the false ideologies of the demoniac (as seen in verse 16.8), now extends the teaching from the plane of erroneous understanding to its grim fruit in action.

Here, the verse presents a piercing portrayal of those who, shackled by a distorted worldview, give rise to destruction—both of themselves and of the world.

— ॐ श्रीरामाय नमः ॐ —

This śloka exposes the full unfolding of āsuric nature: a confluence of delusion, moral decay, and destructive impact.

These individuals, lacking in discernment and anchored in baseless materialism, become agents of disharmony.

Their lives are bereft of dharmic anchorage; their pursuits, ignoble and cruel.

They are absent of śraddhā (faith), blind to the Lord's sovereignty, and dismissive of the eternal soul.

Such people, though they may outwardly prosper or hold worldly power, are destined to be instruments of ruin, caught in a web of their own making, perpetuating a cycle of harm and spiritual darkness all around.

Thus in this verse, Shri Bhagwāna completes the trajectory from misguided dṛṣṭi (vision) to destructive karma (action), underscoring the inexorable link between one's inner convictions and their outer consequences.

—: Key Sanskrit Terms :—

— ॐ तत सत ॐ —

Now let us lean close to the verse's breath and listen—not only with ears, but with the soul's stillness—for in each Sanskrit utterance lies a unlatched door—an open portal to every facet of wiseness; and here we become cognizant of the demonical kind—who are like untamed fire set loose, destroying others and themselves too; and in each syllable we can hear the crackles of ruin that befall those who, void of Dharma, run amuck.

— ॐ —

एतां दृष्टिमवष्टभ्य (Etāṁ dṛṣṭim avaṣṭabhya) – Clinging to this vision:

- दृष्टि Dṛṣṭi means viewpoint, philosophical stance, inner lens.
- अवष्टभ्य Avaṣṭabhya (from स्तम्भ stambh, to support, hold on) means holding tightly, being bound to.

These beings are firmly rooted in the previous verse's worldview—that existence is devoid of Truth, God, and purpose (असत्यं, अनीश्वरम, काम-हैतुकम asatyam, anīśvaram, kāma-haitukam).

It is not a passing idea—it is their foundation.

— ॐ —

नष्टात्मानः (Naṣṭātmānaḥ) – Self-ruined / Lost to the Self:

- आत्मन् Ātman here implies both inner Self and true identity.
- नष्ट Naṣṭa means lost, destroyed.

These beings are disconnected from their own essence, unaware of the सत चित आनन्द sat-cit-ānanda that shines behind the veil of ego.

They live as if the Self does not exist, having fallen into identification with the non-Self (अनात्मा anātman).

— ॐ —

अल्पबुद्धयः (Alpa-buddhayaḥ) – Of little understanding / feeble intellect:
- अल्प Alpa - small;
- बुद्धि buddhi - intellect, discernment.

This is not an insult, but an ontological diagnosis: their buddhi is not sharpened by विवेक viveka (discrimination) or illumined by श्रद्धा śraddhā (faith).

The asuras lack the capacity to inquire into Reality beyond the senses. Theirs is a life fully in the physical domain.

— ॐ —

प्रभवन्ति (Prabhavanti) – They arise / come forth:
Indicates repeated emergence—such beings are reborn again and again, manifesting as forces within संसार saṁsāra that disrupt harmony.

Their rise is not accidental but driven by unresolved संस्कार saṁskāras.

— ॐ —

उग्रकर्माणः (Ugra-karmāṇaḥ) – Engaged in fierce, violent actions:
- उग्र Ugra - intense, cruel, harsh, terrifying.
- कर्म Karma - actions.

These are not ordinary deeds, but actions driven by force, devoid of compassion or higher aim.

These are tamasic and rajasic तामसि राजसि acts—born of lust, anger, and delusion (काम कोध मोह kāma-krodha-moha).

— ॐ —

क्षयाय (Kṣayāya) – For the destruction of...:
Derived from क्ष kṣ (to decay, perish).

The word indicates corrosion, disintegration—not only materially, but morally and spiritually.

— ॐ —

जगतः (Jagataḥ) – Of the world / of living beings:
The āsuric beings are not neutral—they are opposed to the flow of dharma, of harmony and order.

Their influence is adharmic, destabilizing the natural and cosmic rhythms.

— ॐ —

अहिताः (Ahitāḥ) – Malevolent / harmful / hostile:

From अ a- (not) + हित hita (beneficial, friendly, auspicious).

They are foes not just to others, but to the very order of the world.

In denying ईश्वर īśvara, they reject ऋत ṛta, and thus become instruments of disorder.

—: In Brief :—

— ॐ श्रीकृष्णाय नमः ॐ —

Thus, this verse serves as a solemn reminder that the rejection of divine truth and moral law is not a harmless intellectual stance but a gateway to ruinous action.

Holding fast to their perverse doctrines, these deluded beings—bereft of purity, upright conduct, and truthfulness—become veritable enemies of the world -- and of course of themselves as well.

Their vision, corrupted by denial of the soul's eternal nature and the Lord's supreme governance, blinds them to higher purpose and right action.

Fixed in gross material pursuits, they seek fulfillment in fleeting pleasures, unable to perceive the deeper reality that upholds the cosmos.

Their crassly intellect, though cunning in worldly affairs, is barren of spiritual insight; thus, their actions grow ever more violent and heedless, sowing seeds of discord and suffering wherever they tread.

— ॐ श्रीरामाय नमः ॐ —

Such is the grim fate of those mired in āsuric disposition: they sever their link with dharma and squander the precious human birth, becoming instruments of harm to themselves and others.

Yet, the Lord's exposition does not halt here. Having unveiled the inner distortions and outer consequences of the demoniac path, Bhagwāna Shri Krishna in the following verse turns to showcase Minds infested with insatiable desires and of the entanglements which bind them—thus further deepening our understanding of the full measure of thralldoms of the āsuric type.

— ॐ तत सत ॐ —

Before we move on, let us bow in reverence to this sacred verse. Write it by hand, reflect on its meaning, chant it aloud, make it your own.

— ॐ —

एतां दृष्टिमवष्टभ्य नष्टात्मानोऽल्पबुद्धयः ।
etāṁ dṛṣṭimavaṣṭabhya naṣṭātmāno'lpabuddhayaḥ
प्रभवन्त्युग्रकर्माणः क्षयाय जगतोऽहिताः ॥१६-९॥
prabhavantyugrakarmāṇaḥ kṣayāya jagato'hitāḥ (16-9)

— ॐ —

एतां दृष्टिमवष्टभ्य नष्टात्मानोऽल्पबुद्धयः ।
etām dṛṣṭimavaṣṭabhya naṣṭātmāno'lpabuddhayaḥ
प्रभवन्त्युग्रकर्माणः क्षयाय जगतोऽहिताः ॥१६-९॥
prabhavantyugrakarmāṇaḥ kṣayāya jagato'hitāḥ (16-9)

ॐ तत्सदिति श्रीमद्भगवद्गीतासूपनिषत्सु ब्रह्मविद्यायां योगशास्त्रे श्रीकृष्णार्जुनसंवादे
om tatsaditi śrīmadbhagavadgītāsūpaniṣatsu brahmavidyāyāṁ yogaśāstre śrīkṛṣṇārjunasaṁvāde
दैवासुरसम्पद्विभागयोगो नाम षोडशोऽध्यायः श्लोकः ९
daivāsurasampadvibhāgayogo nāma ṣoḍaśo'dhyāyaḥ ślokaḥ 9

Om-Tat-Sat—Om (Braham) is the sole Reality. In the Yogic Scripture on the Science-of-Braham, the Shrimada-Bhāgvada-Gītā Upanishad, we hereby conclude Shloka 9 of the Dialogue between Shrī Krishna and Arjuna entitled Daivāsura-Sampada-Vibhāga-Yoga, Canto XVI.

The Crown of the Beast

Behold, how they have risen—and risen so high.
Clad not in Truth, but in Tech.
With tongues of steel, eyes like spreadsheets,
They have mapped the veins of the earth.
And they call it the Conquest of 'Our' science.
But they stand forgetful of their own self, and whence they came.
They rule the world, keenly watching over all "others"—
Never once remembering their own breath, their Ātmā, their own Self.

A Newly-Made Tree—Immaculate, Sterile, Seedless

Q: What has grown from a soul but denies its own root?
A: Ruling Elites. Industrialists. Systems without souls.

And cities have sprouted—vast and soulless,
Lit by lights that burn nothing; fed by hands that never touch.
Even their hybrid trees, fruits, crops, grains are shaped by algorithms.
But the winds have forgotten how to sing—for they do feel and know:
Of the impeccable slaughter-houses that daily butcher billions—
But Lo -- with not a single blood-drop staining the floor, or man's soul.

Manufactured from Bricks of Destruction—It All Ends with Thy Ruin.
Ye Stand Warned, O Man, Just Watch Out!

The Rulers no longer need no bombs or swords,
The Elites have ensured humanity's destruction is gradual, meticulous —but sure.
Their each advert is a gospel of Want,
Their each inane product adds to man's ritual of forgetting the Self.

The gods of rampant growth demand Sacrifice—
So they feed the masses upon creatures, forests, oceans, earth;
And eventually—and that day is not far away, O mortal—
They will feed upon the very own grandchildren of Thine—
For haven't they already devoured the soul of thy child?

ॐ गीता श्लोकः १६.१० – GĪTĀ VERSE 16.10

ॐ श्रीमद्भगवद्गीतासूपनिषत्सु ब्रह्मविद्यायां योगशास्त्रे श्रीकृष्णार्जुनसंवादे
om śrīmadbhagavadgītāsūpaniṣatsu brahmavidyāyāṁ yogaśāstre śrīkṛṣṇārjunasaṁvāde
दैवासुरसम्पद्विभागयोगो नाम षोडशोऽध्यायः श्लोकः १०
daivāsurasampadvibhāgayogo nāma ṣoḍaśo'dhyāyaḥ ślokaḥ 10

— ॐ —

काममाश्रित्य दुष्पूरं दम्भमानमदान्विताः ।
kāmamāśritya duṣpūraṁ dambhamānamadānvitāḥ
मोहाद्गृहीत्वासद्ग्राहान्प्रवर्तन्तेऽशुचिव्रताः ॥१६-१०॥
mohādgṛhītvāsadgrāhānpravartante'śucivratāḥ (16-10)

Cherishing insatiable desires, embracing false doctrines, full of hypocrisy, pride and arrogance, these demoniacs of impure conduct, persist in this world holding fast to their delusional views. (16.10)

—: Word-by-Word :—

कामम् kāmam – desire; **आश्रित्य** āśritya – resorting to; **दुष्पूरम्** duṣpūram – insatiable; **दम्भम्** dambham – hypocrisy; **मानम्** mānam – pride; **मदान्विताः** mada-anvitāḥ – and arrogance; **मोहात्** mohāt – out of delusion; **गृहीत्वा** gṛhītvā – accepting; **असद्ग्राहान्** asad-grāhān – false views; **प्रवर्तन्ते** pravartante – they act; **अशुचिव्रताः** aśuci-vratāḥ – with impure resolves.

—: Understanding The Verse :—

— ॐ श्रीकृष्णाय नमः ॐ —

In this verse Shri Bhagwāna delves yet more deeply into the anatomy of the āsuric being, turning from the outer wreckage caused by such souls to their own inner world—a realm teeming with ceaseless cravings and delusive pride.

Having established in the previous verses how destructive action springs from erroneous vision, the Lord now illuminates the undercurrents which sustain this ruinous path: unquenchable desires, false doctrines, and full intoxication upon egoic grandeur.

— ॐ श्रीरामाय नमः ॐ —

This verse unveils the inner fortress of the demoniac: built upon hypocrisy, bolstered by arrogance, and cloaked in a veneer of false righteousness.

Such beings are not merely victims of ignorance; they are active participants in the perpetuation of their own bondages, adhering to crooked views and impure conduct—while they flourish--ostensibly.

Their lives are driven by an insatiable hunger—a hunger that, like a fire fed by endless fuel, can never be appeased. By rejecting divine ordinance and spurning the guidance of śāstra and Sanātana-Dharma, they forge a path entirely opposed to the cosmic order.

— ॐ यतिरूपाय नमः ॐ —

Shri Bhagwāna here not only exposes their warped moral compass but also lays bare the spiritual pathology that afflicts them: the delusion that power and pleasure constitute true independence.

Deceived by their transient gains, they exalt themselves in false autonomy, blind to the deeper truth that all beings are held within a divine law.

Over time, their very existence becomes an enactment of falsehood—rooted in delusion, perpetuated through egoism, and culminating in ever-deepening impurity.

—: Key Sanskrit Terms :—

— ॐ तत सत ॐ —

To learn of the demoniac type is like walking midst the hiss of storm-winds. Hypocritical, arrogant, greedy, bound to insatiable desire—each word whips restless and fierce.

But no worries, let us tread as one walks through the fog—not blind, but alert. The Sanskrit expressions here are like trees emerging through the smog, giving form to the formless, helping us know where we stand.

— ॐ —

कामम् आश्रित्य (Kāmam āśritya) – Relying on / taking refuge in desire:

- **काम** Kāma is not merely sensual longing—it is compulsive craving, a fire that never says "enough."
- **आश्रित्य** āśritya means to resort to, depend upon.

The āsuric being is not simply affected by desire—they are rooted in it, governed by it—as a king is by his throne.

Desire becomes their inner refuge, their false deity.

— ॐ —

दुष्पूरं (Duṣpūram) – Insatiable / unfillable:

- From **दुष्** dus- (bad, difficult) and **पूर** pūra (filling, satisfying).

A powerful adjective for **काम** kāma

—a fire that consumes and then keeps consuming without end—
until we ourselves become fully consumed in that fire,
and then the body falls away – dust and ash is all that remains.

— ॐ —

दम्भ-मान-मदान्विताः (Dambha-māna-madānvitāḥ) – Endowed with hypocrisy, vanity, and arrogance:
- दम्भ Dambha: spiritual pretense, false virtue.
- मान Māna: ego-based pride or desire for respect.
- मद् Mada: intoxication, especially with power, wealth, knowledge, or youth.

These three bind the mind to illusion and harden the ego. They are the ornaments of the false self.

— ॐ —

मोहात् (Mohāt) – From delusion:
- मोह Moha is confusion, deluded understanding, a tamasic state in which the Real is mistaken for the non-real, and vice versa.

The source of their entire behavior is not knowledge, but obscuration—they are not acting from clarity, but from inner blindness.

— ॐ —

गृहीत्वा असद्ग्राहान् (Gṛhītvā asad-grāhān) – Grasping false doctrines:
- गृहीत्वा Gṛhītvā - having seized or embraced.
- असद्ग्राह Asad-grāha - असत asad (unreal, false) + ग्राह grāha (grasping, holding).

They cling to false views—intellectually, morally, metaphysically.

These are not neutral errors but attachments to falsehoods that reinforce the web of bondages.

— ॐ —

प्रवर्तन्ते (Pravartante) – They engage / act upon:

Not only do they hold these views, but they act them out, further entrenching their karma and misleading others. There is momentum in their delusion.

— ॐ —

अशुचिव्रताः (Aśuci-vratāḥ) – Vowed to impurity / of impure resolve:
- अशुचि Aśuci - impure, defiled, both morally and spiritually.
- व्रत Vrata - vow, discipline, sacred observance.

Ironically, these beings have their own 'vows', but they are vows of impurity—अधर्मि तप adharmic tapas, performed with pride and desire.

—: In Brief :—

Thus, we behold in this verse a portrait of souls ensnared by their own insatiable cravings, who, far from seeking liberation, entrench themselves further in delusion.

Inflamed by pride and blinded by arrogance, they move through the world beatifying false doctrines and impure resolutions.

Their minds, bereft of higher discernment, cling to Desire alone as the sole axis of life.

The Lord had already declared in the third chapter that Desire, likened to a devouring flame, is never satiated.

— ॐ कौलिनाय नमः ॐ —

Desire is forever consuming—and forever demanding.

To base one's existence upon desire is to drink from a mirage: appearing full yet always empty.

The Manu Smṛti also says:

न जातु कामः कामानामुपभोगेन शाम्यति । हविषा कृष्णवर्त्मैव भूय एवाभिवर्धते ॥२.९४॥

na jātu kāmaḥ kāmānāmupabhogena śāmyati , haviṣā kṛṣṇavartmaiva bhūya evābhivardhate (manu-2.94)

Desire is never extinguished by the enjoyment of desired objects; it only grows stronger like a yajna fire (fed) with clarified butter.

— ॐ पुण्यश्रवणकीर्तनाय नमः ॐ —

Asuric demonic beings, mistaking dependence for freedom, believe themselves sovereign because they possess wealth and power—although they stay fully as slaves to their own lower nature - and are so full of it!

Having no faith in the śāstra, no reverence for the Divine, and no recognition of the soul's true aim, they wander adrift, propelled by impulses and illusions.

They forfeit the guidance of Dharma and find their reference in Desires—with refuge solely in the fleeting pleasures.

In the subsequent verses, Shri Bhagwāna will further unmask the inner workings of such beings—revealing the thoughts that agitate their minds and the corrupt conduct that marks their lives.

The teaching proceeds to unveil the full panorama of the demoniac disposition—and this allows we seekers to discern with ever greater clarity the dangers of deviation from the path of Sanātana-Dharma.

— ॐ तत सत ॐ —

Before we move on, let us bow in reverence to this sacred verse. Write it by hand, reflect on its meaning, chant it aloud, make it your own.

— ॐ —

कामम‍ाश्रित्य दुष्पूरं दम्भमानमदान्विताः ।
kāmamāśritya duṣpūraṁ dambhamānamadānvitāḥ
मोहाद्गृहीत्वासद्ग्राहान्प्रवर्तन्तेऽशुचिव्रताः ॥१६-१०॥
mohādgṛhītvāsadgrāhānpravartante'śucivratāḥ (16-10)

कामम‍ाश्रित्य दुष्पूरं दम्भमानमदान्विताः ।
kāmamāśritya duṣpūraṁ dambhamānamadānvitāḥ
मोहाद्गृहीत्वासद्ग्राहान्प्रवर्तन्तेऽशुचिव्रताः ॥१६-१०॥
mohādgṛhītvāsadgrāhānpravartante'śucivratāḥ (16-10)

ॐ तत्सदिति श्रीमद्भगवद्गीतासूपनिषत्सु ब्रह्मविद्यायां योगशास्त्रे श्रीकृष्णार्जुनसंवादे
om tatsaditi śrīmadbhagavadgītāsūpaniṣatsu brahmavidyāyāṁ yogaśāstre śrīkṛṣṇārjunasaṁvāde
दैवासुरसम्पद्विभागयोगो नाम षोडशोऽध्यायः श्लोकः १०
daivāsurasampadvibhāgayogo nāma ṣoḍaśo'dhyāyaḥ ślokaḥ 10

Om-Tat-Sat—Om (Braham) is the sole Reality. In the Yogic Scripture on the Science-of-Braham, the Shrimada-Bhāgvada-Gītā Upanishad, we hereby conclude Shloka 10 of the Dialogue between Shrī Krishna and Arjuna entitled Daivāsura-Sampada-Vibhāga-Yoga, Canto XVI.

Tale of Macaulay's Macullūs— Modern-Day Asuras.

He spurns Dharma's Light—
Cherishes hunger though -- nurses it Proud,
He calls it march, progress, power, growth.
His ancestors taught: All is Braham, everything is alive, all have souls.
Now he revels in trillions-dollars economies, Beef-exports.

He has whipped Corruption and Hunger to a Fine Art
Consuming everything around, finally he devours his own soul—
Staring back from the mirror—now just a worthless soulless shadow.

The Blinded Masses of False Vision, Distorted Beliefs

In shadowed corners, where truth stays concealed,
He flails his arms to grasp at mystery, miracle, unseen—
But with Dharma Shastras thrown away, his heart stay unhealed.

Blind to Dharma's light, he wanders through the haze,
Cursing the dawn, while lost in a shadowy maze.

In *विपरीत ज्ञान* viparīta jñāna , he dwells and weeps,
Mind wrapped in delusion, lost in sleep.

With soul's wisdom veiled, his body robbed of youth,
Clasping a deluding world bequeathed by his western Asura-Masters—
The wannabe, the little asura, calls it the New-Religion, New-Truth.

Like blind men claiming "Darkness is the Sun",
He flees the Sanatana Light *सनातन धर्म*, before it has even begun.

ॐ गीता श्लोकः १६.११ – GĪTĀ VERSE 16.11

ॐ श्रीमद्भगवद्गीतासूपनिषत्सु ब्रह्मविद्यायां योगशास्त्रे श्रीकृष्णार्जुनसंवादे
om śrīmadbhagavadgītāsūpaniṣatsu brahmavidyāyāṁ yogaśāstre śrīkṛṣṇārjunasaṁvāde
दैवासुरसम्पद्विभागयोगो नाम षोडशोऽध्यायः श्लोकः ११
daivāsurasampadvibhāgayogo nāma ṣoḍaśo'dhyāyaḥ ślokaḥ 11

— ॐ —

चिन्तामपरिमेयां च प्रलयान्तामुपाश्रिताः ।
cintāmaparimeyāṁ ca pralayāntāmupāśritāḥ
कामोपभोगपरमा एतावदिति निश्चिताः ॥१६-११॥
kāmopabhogaparamā etāvaditi niścitāḥ (16-11)

Beset with innumerable cares—which end only with their deaths—they remain devoted to the enjoyment of sensuous pleasures, convinced that this is all there is to it, firm in their belief that this is the highest limit of joy. (16.11)

—: Word-by-Word :—

चिन्ताम् cintām – anxiety; **अपरिमेयाम्** aparimeyām – immeasurable; **च** ca – and; **प्रलयान्ताम्** pralayāntām – ending only with death; **उपाश्रिताः** upāśritāḥ – having embraced; **कामोपभोगपरमाः** kāma-upabhoga-paramāḥ – considering sensual enjoyment as the highest goal; **एतावत्** etāvat – this alone; **इति** iti – thus; **निश्चिताः** niścitāḥ – are convinced.

—: Understanding The Verse :—

— ॐ श्रीकृष्णाय नमः ॐ —

In Bhagavad-Gītā 16.11, Shri Bhagwāna draws us yet further into the inner chambers of the āsuric existence, unfolding the ceaseless agitation and inward turmoil that accompany a life misaligned with Sanātana-Dharma.

Having earlier depicted the false doctrines and arrogant dispositions that shape the external lives of such souls, the Lord now unveils their inner climate—a state not of peace but of relentless anxiety and unslakable craving.

This verse marks a transition from outer action to inner bondage, exposing how a being, cut off from higher truth, becomes an arrant prisoner to worries and worldly concerns.

— ॐ रामेश्वराय नमः ॐ —

Here, Shri Bhagwāna reveals the pitiable plight of those who, driven by material ambition and blind pursuit of pleasure, become ensnared in a web of endless cares.

Their thoughts are perpetually occupied with acquisition, preservation, and indulgence, and their lives are consumed by the feverish quest for sensual satisfaction.

They mistake this fleeting joy for the pinnacle of human fulfillment, wholly dismissing the soul's deeper yearning for the eternal.

Rooted in avidyā (ignorance), they fail to discern that all objects of pleasure are transient and that no amount of worldly attainment can satiate the immortal spirit.

In this way, the Lord allows us to witness not merely the outward decadence of the āsuric nature, but its inward poverty: a restless striving that ends only with death, leaving the soul bereft of the true joy that comes from alignment with the Divine.

Lo, from thousands of years ago the spoken words of Bhagwāna Shri Krishna have reached us this day—and which so aptly describe the modern-day man.

—: Key Sanskrit Terms :—

— ॐ तत सत ॐ —

The life of asuras is a tangled net, with no abiding happiness anywhere—blips of fleeting delights, hopping from one to next, is their only lot in life.

Endless anxieties, desires insatiable, caught in delusion, their every day coils around their neck, binding them ever tighter.

Not a pretty picture; but still, let us peer into the Sanskrit terms of the verse—enter the labyrinth of language -- alike an entry into mirror and maze -- where each term leads inward, and every turn is both an exit and new entrance.

— ॐ —

चिन्ताम् (Cintām) – Anxiety / care / worry:

चिन्ता Cintā denotes deep mental agitation, the gnawing concern that dominates one's mind when it is tethered to the fleeting and impermanent.

Mind it: this is not noble contemplation (**मनन** manana), but the restless churning of the mind in fear and attachments.

— ॐ —

अपरिमेयां (Aparimeyām) – Incalculable / boundless:

The words is from the roots **अ** a- (not), **परि** pari- (around), and **मेय** meya (measured): of un-measured extent.

These worries are immeasurable, infinite, because they are based on insatiable desires.

A life anchored in काम kāma breeds endless agitations—and is a life bereft of peace.

— ॐ —

प्रलयान्ताम् (Pralayāntām) – Ending only in death:

प्रलय Pralaya - dissolution, death.

These anxieties do not cease until the very end of life—and not even then... for the next rebirth follows.

Their mental suffering has no reprieve, no contentment, because it is fueled by desires that are दुष्पूर duṣpūra (insatiable).

— ॐ —

उपाश्रिताः (Upāśritāḥ) – Taking refuge in / clinging to:

These beings do not merely experience anxiety—they have now come to depend upon it – as their very necessary ecosystem, as though it were the natural condition of life.

They are enmeshed in it, having no higher foundation.

— ॐ —

काम-उपभोग-परमाः (Kāma-upabhoga-paramāḥ) – Supremely devoted to desire and enjoyment:

- काम Kāma - desire.
- उपभोग Upabhoga - enjoyment, indulgence.
- परमाः Paramāḥ - considering this to be the highest, ultimate.

For them, pleasure is the highest goal, the supreme pursuit. Their entire life is bhoga-mārga, the path of enjoyment, devoid of spiritual insight or renunciation.

— ॐ —

एतावत् इति निश्चिताः (Etāvat iti niścitāḥ) – Convinced that this is all:

- एतावत् Etāvat - this alone, nothing beyond.
- इति निश्चिताः Iti niścitāḥ - firmly decided, having concluded thus.

They are mentally firm—obstinate—in their belief that material pleasure is all that life is about.

In their worldview, there is no higher joy, no innate bliss of the Self, no transcendence—only more consumption and an endless hunger, chasing each other in a vicious circle.

—: In Brief :—

— ॐ श्रीकृष्णाय नमः ॐ —

Thus, these deluded souls, surrendering themselves to innumerable anxieties—which stretch unbroken until the very hour of their death—devote their entire existence to the pursuit of sensual enjoyments.

They are firmly anchored in the belief that worldly pleasure is the ultimate summit of human aspiration, mistaking the flickering for the eternal, and the perishable for the imperishable.

The Lord's words here lay bare the tragic irony of such a life: in seeking fulfillment through the ever-changing, they find themselves endlessly restless, their desires multiplying like a fire fed by fresh fuel.

— ॐ कृष्णाय वासुदेवाय नमः ॐ —

Their anxious toil, far from granting peace, binds them deeper into the snares of saṃsāra.

Blinded by attachment and intoxicated by worldly prosperity, they become incapable of perceiving either the illusory nature of the world or the presence of the Divine.

Their gaze remains firmly fixed upon the material plane, and thus, the soul—whose true nature is unstilted natural bliss—remains veiled, forgotten amid the clamor of insistent riffling desires.

In the next verse, Shri Bhagwāna will deepen this portrait further—revealing how these beings further entangle themselves in elaborate schemes and ambitions, driven by an insatiable thirst for power and possession. The chain of delusion tightens, as their actions grow ever more feverish and their vision ever more obscured.

Let us read on—and let us stay warned to never stray that way.

— ॐ तत सत ॐ —

Before we move on, let us bow in reverence to this sacred verse—a timeless beacon of wisdom guiding seekers for ages. Write it by hand, reflect on its meaning, and chant it aloud, for these sounds alone carry the authenticity of that era. The world may have changed but the living vibration of these Sanskrit sounds still remain as original as they were when Bhagwān Shri Krishna Himself walked the earth and imparted these teachings.

— ॐ —

चिन्तामपरिमेयां च प्रलयान्तामुपाश्रिताः ।
cintāmaparimeyāṁ ca pralayāntāmupāśritāḥ
कामोपभोगपरमा एतावदिति निश्चिताः ॥१६-११॥
kāmopabhogaparamā etāvaditi niścitāḥ (16-11)

— ॐ —
चिन्तामपरिमेयां च प्रलयान्तामुपाश्रिताः ।
cintāmaparimeyāṁ ca pralayāntāmupāśritāḥ
कामोपभोगपरमा एतावदिति निश्चिताः ॥१६-११॥
kāmopabhogaparamā etāvaditi niścitāḥ (16-11)

ॐ तत्सदिति श्रीमद्भगवद्गीतासूपनिषत्सु ब्रह्मविद्यायां योगशास्त्रे श्रीकृष्णार्जुनसंवादे
om tatsaditi śrīmadbhagavadgītāsūpaniṣatsu brahmavidyāyāṁ yogaśāstre śrīkṛṣṇārjunasaṁvāde
दैवासुरसम्पद्विभागयोगो नाम षोडशोऽध्यायः श्लोकः ११
daivāsurasampadvibhāgayogo nāma ṣoḍaśo'dhyāyaḥ ślokaḥ 11

Om-Tat-Sat—Om (Braham) is the sole Reality. In the Yogic Scripture on the Science-of-Braham, the Shrimada-Bhāgvada-Gītā Upanishad, we hereby conclude Shloka 11 of the Dialogue between Shrī Krishna and Arjuna entitled Daivāsura-Sampada-Vibhāga-Yoga, Canto XVI.

O My Mind, What Coils of Thoughts Constrict Thee So?
अनेक चिन्ता Anêka-cintâ—Alas, my thoughts are not wings but weights.
They do not lift me to God; They bind me to baseless Fears.
This plan, that fear, this loss, that gain...
Each day I wake—a slave to uncertainty.

I count my gold, then recount it in doubt;
I worry my pleasures will leave, be snatched—or my children & spouse.
And when they stay, I worry still.
O my soul, how did worry become thy daily worship?

O Mind, Why thy Peace is always in "When... & After..."—never Now?
"After I get this, I shall have it made... and then I'll rest..."
"When this event comes to pass... then I shall rejoice..."
Thusly I promise each night—only to break that promise each day.
I run. And I run. And I run.
But the finish line moves further—or it is I who push it down.
Alas, it looks like the end of worry is not in success,
but only in Death—प्रलयान्ताम Pralayântâm.
And perhaps not even then—for one never really dies,
In Death, misery merely changes shape—returns donning new skin.

O fool, Anxiety is the Echo of Ego. But Thou art Not Ego—but the **âtmâ**.
Aye, there Is something more than this—
More than this skin, more than wealth, status, people, love, kin.
There is the stillness of sages, the bliss of those who know the Self—
—the Âtmâ. Unborn. Unmade. Closer than breath. Older than Space

---

Thou seekest happiness in objects, in lovers, in things which die/rot.
While the Ocean of Bliss undulates—right behind thy brow.

O mortal, Go—become anchored to that Satya again,
Drinking from the well of Gitâ-śâstra—live steadfast in Sanâtana-Dharma.

ॐ गीता श्लोकः १६.१२ – GĪTĀ VERSE 16.12

ॐ श्रीमद्भगवद्गीतासूपनिषत्सु ब्रह्मविद्यायां योगशास्त्रे श्रीकृष्णार्जुनसंवादे
om śrīmadbhagavadgītāsūpaniṣatsu brahmavidyāyāṁ yogaśāstre śrīkṛṣṇārjunasaṁvāde
दैवासुरसम्पद्विभागयोगो नाम षोडशोऽध्यायः श्लोकः १२
daivāsurasampadvibhāgayogo nāma ṣoḍaśo'dhyāyaḥ ślokaḥ 12

— ॐ —

आशापाशशतैर्बद्धाः कामक्रोधपरायणाः ।
āśāpāśaśatairbaddhāḥ kāmakrodhaparāyaṇāḥ
ईहन्ते कामभोगार्थमन्यायेनार्थसञ्चयान् ॥१६-१२॥
īhante kāmabhogārthamanyāyenārthasañcayān (16-12)

Bound by innumerable ties of expectations and given to lust and anger, they strive to amass through foul means piles of riches—only for the purpose of sense-gratifications. (16.12)

—: Word-by-Word :—

आशापाशशतैः āśā-pāśa-śataiḥ – by hundreds of fetters of hope; **बद्धाः** baddhāḥ – bound; **कामक्रोधपरायणाः** kāma-krodha-parāyaṇāḥ – devoted to desire and anger; **ईहन्ते** īhante – they strive; **कामभोगार्थम्** kāma-bhoga-artham – for sensual enjoyment; **अन्यायेन** anyāyena – through unjust means; **अर्थसञ्चयान्** artha-sañcayān – accumulation of wealth.

—: Understanding The Verse :—

— ॐ श्रीकृष्णाय नमः ॐ —

Verse 16.12 continues the unabashed revelation of the **आसुरी भाव** āsuric bhāva, painting an even more horrific picture—depicting how the inner unrest of anxious desire (as seen in 16.11) lead one to the outward entanglements and corrupt pursuits -- which ensue inevitably from such unrest.

Here Bhagwāna Shri Krishna vividly portrays how these beings—shackled by ceaseless expectations and propelled by lust and anger—immerse themselves in schemes of accumulation and exploitation, their lives a tangle of restless striving and moral decay.

— ॐ श्रीरामाय नमः ॐ —

The Lord unmasks the chains that bind the demoniac: an unbroken web of hopes, cravings, and schemes, pursued not for any higher end but solely for sensual gratifications.

These individuals, seeing no higher principle than self-indulgence, give themselves wholly to काम kāma (desire) and क्रोध krodha (anger)—the twin forces that drive them deeper into bondages.

Wealth becomes not a means of Gītā-Dharma service or Dharmic fulfillment, but an end in itself, amassed without scruple through deceit, exploitation, and violence—accumulated in frenzy, but not really knowing why.

Their vision is narrowed to just the pursuit of physical pleasures, their minds clouded by the delusion which makes them believe that power and possession will secure lasting joy.

— ॐ सीतापतये नमः ॐ —

Bound by hope, lust, desire, they fall to cruel means. Each day strains at them harsh and unrelenting.

Lust and desires is like cords pulled taut around their necks—slowly, but surely, strangulating them.

And yet, within this grim portrayal lies a silent reminder of the soul's inherent freedom: these bonds are self-forged and may, by grace and right effort, be broken.

The verse serves both as a warning and a call to clarity—a vivid depiction of saṁsāra's snares, urging all seekers to recognize and transcend the enticements that bind the soul to sufferings.

—: Key Sanskrit Terms :—

— ॐ तत सत ॐ —

Now let us walk the twilight corridors of this verse, where each Sanskrit utterance gleams like dew upon the leaf of understanding.

— ॐ —

आशापाशशतैः (Āśā-pāśa-śataiḥ) – By hundreds of ropes of expectation:
- आशा Āśā - hope, longing, expectation (especially for future enjoyment).
- पाश Pāśa - cord, fetter, snare.
- शत Śata - hundred, denoting abundance.

These beings are not free agents; they are entangled in a web of imagined future pleasures, each hope a पाश pāśa—a noose binding the soul to संसार saṁsāra.

The mind projects endlessly: "I will be happy when..."—but alas, that "when" event never comes to pass -- keeps getting pushed further down.

— ॐ —

बद्धाः (Baddhāḥ) – Bound / tied:

A stark word!

These souls are not merely influenced, but bound, as by chains—not by external forces, but by the cords of their own craving.

The Self, though inherently free, has become veiled and imprisoned —by webs of its own making.

— ॐ —

कामक्रोधपरायणाः (Kāma-krodha-parāyaṇāḥ) – Devoted to lust and anger:

- काम Kāma - desire.
- क्रोध Krodha - anger, born from obstructed desire.
- परायण Parāyaṇa - devoted to, taking refuge in.

These are not occasional visitors but the principle gods in the life of such people—and they stay devoted to them.

— ॐ —

ईहन्ते (Īhante) – They strive / endeavor intensely:

From the root ईह īh—to strive, to desire earnestly. Their effort is real, but misdirected.

This shows that energy, initiative, and ambition—divorced from discernment विवेक (viveka)—become forces of bondage.

— ॐ —

कामभोगार्थम् (Kāma-bhoga-artham) – For the sake of sensual enjoyment:

Their striving is not for dharma, not for the simple natural welfare of their own body, not for Self-realization—but solely to feed the fire of the senses.

The very opposite of yoga-mārga, योग मार्ग this is the भोग मार्ग bhoga-mārga—the path of indulgence, ever hungry, never sated.

— ॐ —

अन्यायेन (Anyāyena) – By unjust means:

- न्याय Nyāya - righteousness, justice, lawful path.
- अन्याय Anyāya - the opposite—wrongful, dishonest, or adharmic means.

Their commitment to pleasure is so absolute that they do not hesitate to transgress dharma. Ethics are sacrificed at the altar of goddess Desire.

— ॐ —

अर्थसञ्चयान् (Artha-sañcayān) – Accumulation of wealth / piles of possessions:

- अर्थ Artha - wealth, material prosperity.

- सञ्चय Sañcaya - hoarding, gathering, piling up.

Their energy is poured into acquisition, but this wealth is neither offered, nor shared, nor sanctified through Dharma—it is hoarded, driven by insecurity and greed.

—: In Brief :—

— ॐ श्रीकृष्णाय नमः ॐ —

Thus, the demoniac, bound by innumerable strands of hope and craving, surrenders themselves entirely to the pursuit of sensual pleasure, their lives a ceaseless storm of desires which keep shifting and multiplying without end.

Like a moth drawn from one flame to another, their mind flits incessantly from scheme to scheme—first absorbed in one worldly aim, then, without pause, grasping at another, never resting, never fulfilled.

This restless bondage is captured in the Lord's phrase आशापाशशतैर्बद्धाः āśāpāśa-śatair baddhāḥ—bound by hundreds of cords of expectation, their entire existence enslaved to the demands of desire.

— ॐ सर्वदेवस्तुताय नमः ॐ —

Mind it, for these souls, काम क्रोध kāma, krodha etc., are not passing impulses but become their supreme guiding forces—their false dharma, their only recourse.

काम क्रोध kāma, krodha are natural; and they do come visiting as occasional callers in most people's lives. And yet, for the demoniac type, these are not just the occasional visitors—rather the exact opposite; they are the central deities having a permanent place in the parlor of such people's life.

They stay governed—even possessed—by these two शत्रु स्वरूप śatru-svarūpīs—internal enemies identified in the Gītā verse 3.37 as रजोगुणसमुद्भवः rajoguṇa-born obstructions to liberation:

काम एष क्रोध एष रजोगुणसमुद्भवः kāma eṣa krodha eṣa rajoguṇasamudbhavaḥ...

Shri Bhagwāna said: "It is ire and desire—begotten of the elements of Rājas, insatiable and grossly wicked—which are to be regarded as the culprits here: the veritable foes. (3.37)

— ॐ कौसलेयाय नमः ॐ —

The actions of these people, springing from these dark roots, naturally turn toward crooked means: deceit, thefts—direct or subtle, violence, and every manner of injustice -- which are embraced since they serve the aim of amassing more wealth and feeding sensual indulgences.

Such a life, devoid of higher principle, is inevitably self-corrupting and destructive, binding these soul ever tighter in the chains of saṁsāra.

— ॐ विजयाय नमः ॐ —

As the Lord has elsewhere declared (Gītā 2.41), the minds of those lacking in steadiness are scattered, their pursuits endlessly branching and unrooted.

व्यवसायात्मिका बुद्धिरेकेह कुरुनन्दन । बहुशाखा ह्यनन्ताश्च बुद्धयोऽव्यवसायिनाम् ॥२-४१॥
vyavasāyātmikā buddhirekeha kurunandana,
bahuśākhā hyanantāśca buddhayo'vyavasāyinām (2-41)
In this blessed path, O Kurū-Nandana, the intellect abides determinate and concentrated—with a single one-pointed purpose; whereas, the efforts of the irresolute lie scattered all over, wandering undecidedly in infinite directions. (2.41)

— ॐ रुक्मिणीवल्लभाय नमः ॐ —

The āsuric beings, by investing ultimate value in the perishable, forfeit all hope of true peace and fulfillment.

Though they may temporarily control others through force, coercion, anger, or accumulate wealth through cunning, these gains are fragile, doomed to collapse—just as the object of anger, when freed from its grip, will in time retaliate, like a spring uncoiled.

Thus, the fruits of such striving are bitter and fleeting.

In the verses that follow, Shri Bhagwāna will unveil the inner fabric of their imagination and the delusional visions that fuel their ceaseless striving, offering us a deeper glimpse into the mental architecture of the demoniac heart.

— ॐ तत सत ॐ —

Before we move on, let us bow in reverence to this sacred verse. Write it by hand, reflect on its meaning, chant it aloud, make it your own.

— ॐ —

आशापाशशतैर्बद्धाः कामक्रोधपरायणाः ।
āśāpāśaśatairbaddhāḥ kāmakrodhaparāyaṇāḥ
ईहन्ते कामभोगार्थमन्यायेनार्थसञ्चयान् ॥१६-१२॥
īhante kāmabhogārthamanyāyenārthasañcayān (16-12)

— ॐ —

आशापाशशतैर्बद्धाः कामक्रोधपरायणाः ।
āśāpāśaśatairbaddhāḥ kāmakrodhaparāyaṇāḥ
ईहन्ते कामभोगार्थमन्यायेनार्थसञ्चयान् ॥१६-१२॥
īhante kāmabhogārthamanyāyenārthasañcayān (16-12)

ॐ तत्सदिति श्रीमद्भगवद्गीतासूपनिषत्सु ब्रह्मविद्यायां योगशास्त्रे श्रीकृष्णार्जुनसंवादे
om tatsaditi śrīmadbhagavadgītāsūpaniṣatsu brahmavidyāyāṁ yogaśāstre śrīkṛṣṇārjunasaṁvāde
दैवासुरसम्पद्विभागयोगो नाम षोडशोऽध्यायः श्लोकः १२
daivāsurasampadvibhāgayogo nāma ṣoḍaśo'dhyāyaḥ ślokaḥ 12

Om-Tat-Sat—Om (Braham) is the sole Reality. In the Yogic Scripture on the Science-of-Braham, the Shrimada-Bhāgvada-Gītā Upanishad, we hereby conclude Shloka 12 of the Dialogue between Shrī Krishna and Arjuna entitled Daivāsura-Sampada-Vibhāga-Yoga, Canto XVI.

A Hundredfold आशा पाश शत Grueling Chains of Viṣâda विशाद

I wove my hopes from threads of Want and Will आशा पाश—
शत Hundreds of cords—now each pulling me apart.
One promise led to ten, and ten to the whole raging fire—
Each shinier lie eclipsing wisdom's arc.

Now I chase, I grasp, I crave, I rage, I fall—
Yet, there's no rest, no root, no refuge from my unsated thirst.
My hands stay ever full, And with ample hands I gorge
Yet just more-hunger rules my starving days and famished nights,
I stay spinning more dreams—that end up binding my Self more.
And where once was sky, now exist prison walls—I myself forged.

O fire within, why dost thou burn me as lust and rage?

Alas! I am Kâma-krodha-parâyaṇâh कामक्रोधपरायणाः.
No, I do not let in lust and anger any longer—
Because they have already made a permanent throne in my chest.
I desire—and it devours. I am denied—and in my ire I destroy.
My joy is conditional. My rage, irrational.
O fire, thou wast meant for yajña—
Why dost thou now scorch My clarity to ash?

Hope: "The Shining Sword of Sanâtani Jnâna"

But even now, O heart, thou art not lost—
These chains are false, though tightly wrapped they seem.
Desire, though fierce—is fed by thine own Mind,
Withdraw thy will—and see the whole hokum collapse.

The Lord resides beyond these forms & names, smoke & flame,
In stillness He waits—for thy signal to lift thee into realm of Bliss.
Remember: One breath of Truth will incinerate a hundred lies,
One still gaze of Krishna—can still a raging sea of desires.
Come Mortal: cut Hope's delusions in one swift stroke—
Cut all Desires with the shining Sword-of-Bliss.

ॐ गीता श्लोकः १६.१३ – GĪTĀ VERSE 16.13

ॐ श्रीमद्भगवद्गीतासूपनिषत्सु ब्रह्मविद्यायां योगशास्त्रे श्रीकृष्णार्जुनसंवादे
om śrīmadbhagavadgītāsūpaniṣatsu brahmavidyāyāṁ yogaśāstre śrīkṛṣṇārjunasaṁvāde
दैवासुरसम्पद्विभागयोगो नाम षोडशोऽध्यायः श्लोकः १३
daivāsurasampadvibhāgayogo nāma ṣoḍaśo'dhyāyaḥ ślokaḥ 13

— ॐ —

इदमद्य मया लब्धमिमं प्राप्स्ये मनोरथम् ।
idamadya mayā labdhamimaṁ prāpsye manoratham
इदमस्तीदमपि मे भविष्यति पुनर्धनम् ॥१६-१३॥
idamastīdamapi me bhaviṣyati punardhanam (16-13)

Full of desires they say, 'This much I have secured today, and now I shall acquire that; this much wealth is already mine, and soon that yonder too shall be mine. (16.13)

—: Word-by-Word :—

इदम् idam – this; **अद्य** adya – today; **मया** mayā – by me; **लब्धम्** labdham – has been gained; **इमम्** imam – this; **प्राप्स्ये** prāpsye – I shall achieve; **मनोरथम्** manoratham – desire; **इदम्** idam – this; **अस्ति** asti – is; **इदम्** idam – this; **अपि** api – also; **मे** me – mine; **भविष्यति** bhaviṣyati – will be; **पुनः** punaḥ – again; **धनम्** dhanam – wealth.

—: Understanding The Verse :—

— ॐ श्रीकृष्णाय नमः ॐ —

With this verse Shri Bhagwāna takes us inside the very citadel of the āsuric mind—allowing us to overhear the private musings that govern its existence.

No longer are we observing from without, but now we are given direct access to the inner monologue—the stream of thought shaped by insatiable desire, self-centered pride, and the illusion of mastery over destiny.

This verse unveils the heartbeat of the demoniac: an endless cycle of acquisition, anticipation, and attachment, where the soul is trapped in a ceaseless quest for ever more.

— ॐ श्रीरामाय नमः ॐ —

Here, the Lord discloses the self-talk of the one enthralled by material success: "I have gained this today; soon I shall gain that..."

Such thoughts reflect not just normal ambition, but a deeper spiritual malady—a life wholly oriented toward accumulation, where the mind is perpetually projecting itself into imagined futures of increased wealth and expanded possessions.

These beings equate their worth and security with what they own, measuring life's meaning through the lens of external gains.

— ॐ शाश्वताय नमः ॐ —

Yet, beneath this confident exterior lies a profound vulnerability, for all such boasts rest on the fragile foundation of transient materiality.

In contrast to the wise, who may use wealth as a tool for dharmic action—remaining inwardly unattached—these beings are wholly ensnared -- mistaking impermanent treasures for ultimate fulfillment, as their only goal in life.

This verse does not just describe greed, it reveals the deep-seated delusion that blinds one to the eternal, chaining the soul to the ever-receding horizon of worldly desire.

"This I gained, this I shall gain again," the voice of self intoxicated; each syllable swells with pride, hollow yet loud.

—: Key Sanskrit Terms :—

— ॐ तत सत ॐ —

Let us behold this verse as an edifice of language, and let's enter through its Sanskrit doors—each opening to a chamber of deeper insight, each word a footstep upon the path of ancient wisdom.

— ॐ —

इदमद्य मया लब्धम् (Idam adya mayā labdham) – This today has been gained by me:

- **इदम्** Idam - this, referring to a gain or possession.
- **अद्य** Adya - today, immediately, now.
- **मया** Mayā - by me (the egoic agent).
- **लब्धम्** Labdham - obtained, acquired.

The tone is triumphant, self-congratulatory. 'O look at me!'

The āsuric being is intoxicated by acquisition, attributing it solely to his own power, devoid of gratitude or surrender to the Divine—from whom all existence is.

The ego claims all success: "I am the doer; I am the enjoyer." Wow!

— ॐ —

इमं प्राप्स्ये मनोरथम् (Imaṁ prāpsye manoratham) – This desire I shall fulfill next:

- इमं Imaṁ - this (future aim).
- प्राप्स्ये Prāpsye - I shall attain, I will gain.
- मनोरथ Manoratha - heart's wish, mental fantasy, ambition.

The mind is not content with what has been gained—it is already galloping ahead, fixated on the next desire. This is संकल्प saṅkalpa, the ceaseless stream of imagined enjoyments that enslave the mind.

— ॐ —

इदमस्ति (Idam asti) – This I already have:

A reiteration, emphasizing possessiveness. The tone reflects clinging, ममाया mamāyā—"this is mine." Ownership becomes identity.

— ॐ —

इदं अपि मे भविष्यति (Idam api me bhaviṣyati) – That too shall soon be mine:

- अपि Api - also, in addition.
- मे Me - mine.
- भविष्यति Bhaviṣyati - will become.

The being is always projecting into the future, imagining possessions as already half-acquired. This is the illusion of control over the flow of time and karma.

— ॐ —

पुनः धनम् (Punaḥ dhanam) – More and more wealth:

- धनम् Dhanam - wealth.
- पुनः Punaḥ - again, repeatedly, anew.

Alas, his hunger is endless. Each acquisition leads to a new craving.

There is no contentment संतुष्टी (santuṣṭi), only the addiction of accumulation.

Such luckless beings stay so terribly caught in the world!

—: In Brief :—

— ॐ श्रीकृष्णाय नमः ॐ —

In this verse, we see the demoniac being caught in an endless dialogue of self-congratulation and future scheming: "This I have attained; that too shall soon be mine." The Lord, with subtle precision, exposes the workings of a mind intoxicated by मनोरथ manoratha—the chariot of desires that endlessly roams the fields of wealth, power, and sensory satisfaction.

Here, the 'I' and 'mine' अहम मम (aham and mama) stand as twin pillars upholding their inner edifice of delusion.

— ॐ श्रीरामाय नमः ॐ —

Such souls attribute all their past achievements to their own might, bereft of any recognition of the divine order or grace that governs the cosmos.

Their faith is not in Dharma, nor in the providence of **ईश्वर** Īśvara, but in their own effort and cunning. They regard themselves as the architects of their fortune, oblivious to the transient nature of worldly gains and the unseen hand that turns the wheel of destiny.

This verse offers a mirror to the dangers of unchecked ambition, reminding us that even when worldly desires are momentarily fulfilled, they breed yet more longings.

The demoniac, therefore, remains perpetually unfulfilled, driven by the false conviction that satisfaction lies just beyond the next acquisition.

Aye—it's always just beyond; let me just have that and I shall be happiness personified and I shall have it made. Ah, what a fool!

— ॐ पुण्यश्रवणकीर्तनाय नमः ॐ —

In the verses that follow, Shri Bhagwāna will deepen this revelation, showing how such beings weave ever more elaborate webs of expectation and delusion, and how these tangled aspirations shape their ultimate downfall.

Thusly, the teachings of this chapter unfold—warning all sincere seekers of the subtle snares that bind the soul to the miseries of saṁsāra.

— ॐ तत सत ॐ —

Before moving on, let us once more bow in deep reverence before this sacred verse of the Bhagavad-Gītā, an eternal beacon of wisdom that ceaselessly illumines the path of seekers. Engage with its form—inscribe it with your own hand, let your heart dwell upon its meaning, and raise your voice in its chanting—for within these syllables echoes the undying proclamation delivered millennia ago on the battlefield of Kurukshetra. These words, transmitted unchanged across the unbroken chain of generations, form a living bridge, linking us to that sanctified era when Bhagwāna Shri Krishna Himself walked this earth and bestowed this divine teaching. Through the luminous vibration of these sacred Sanskrit sounds, we are drawn nearer to His timeless presence, touching the very heartbeat of the Eternal.

— ॐ —

इदमद्य मया लब्धमिमं प्राप्स्ये मनोरथम् ।

idamadya mayā labdhamimaṁ prāpsye manoratham

इदमस्तीदमपि मे भविष्यति पुनर्धनम् ॥१६-१३॥

idamastīdamapi me bhaviṣyati punardhanam (16-13)

— ॐ —

इदमद्य मया लब्धमिमं प्राप्स्ये मनोरथम् ।
idamadya mayā labdhamimaṁ prāpsye manoratham
इदमस्तीदमपि मे भविष्यति पुनर्धनम् ॥१६-१३॥
idamastīdamapi me bhaviṣyati punardhanam (16-13)

ॐ तत्सदिति श्रीमद्भगवद्गीतासूपनिषत्सु ब्रह्मविद्यायां योगशास्त्रे श्रीकृष्णार्जुनसंवादे
om tatsaditi śrīmadbhagavadgītāsūpaniṣatsu brahmavidyāyāṁ yogaśāstre śrīkṛṣṇārjunasaṁvāde
दैवासुरसम्पद्विभागयोगो नाम षोडशोऽध्यायः श्लोकः १३
daivāsurasampadvibhāgayogo nāma ṣoḍaśo'dhyāyaḥ ślokaḥ 13

Om-Tat-Sat—Om (Braham) is the sole Reality. In the Yogic Scripture on the Science-of-Braham, the Shrimada-Bhāgvada-Gītā Upanishad, we hereby conclude Shloka 13 of the Dialogue between Shrī Krishna and Arjuna entitled Daivāsura-Sampada-Vibhāga-Yoga, Canto XVI.

"I am rich, kingly, powerful. Who here is like me?"
—So cries the clown-of-clay, painted gold in praise.
Surrounded by lackeys, grabbers, contenders, he has no kindred,
He walks not in Dharma,
But on the scaffolding of self-congratulations.

"I am surrounded with wealth, family, ties", he likes to think,
Surrounded—yes—but unloved he truly lives.
Joys bartered, favors traded, laughter rehearsed, his life a theatre,
Every bouquet received—made of anticipations, returns, expectations.

"I will gain more. I will rise even Higher..."
He knows not: the ladder he climbs leans on thin air.
Each rung he climbs, takes him far—
Far—from soul, from sanity, peace, silence,
Farther away from the inborn bliss of Âtmâ—his innate Self.

He owns many things—but has no time to visit or touch.
He Touches—but does not feel.
He Holds—but never sees,
For his eyes are only looking forward to the next conquest.

"Soon, that too shall be mine"—says he;
But behind him—Death laughs low and softly.
His within Self, the Âtmâ, sighs—unneeded, unloved, unseen—
as he keeps running past peace—to grasp at crying & weeping.

Each "mine"—is a stone upon his back,
Each "more"—a tear in his soul,
Brain-dead, the fool builds vacuous towers mimicking after others—
And he calls the Rat-Race: Life's Purpose.

ॐ गीता श्लोकः १६.१४ – GĪTĀ VERSE 16.14

ॐ श्रीमद्भगवद्गीतासूपनिषत्सु ब्रह्मविद्यायां योगशास्त्रे श्रीकृष्णार्जुनसंवादे
om śrīmadbhagavadgītāsūpaniṣatsu brahmavidyāyāṁ yogaśāstre śrīkṛṣṇārjunasaṁvāde
दैवासुरसम्पद्विभागयोगो नाम षोडशोऽध्यायः श्लोकः १४
daivāsurasampadvibhāgayogo nāma ṣoḍaśo'dhyāyaḥ ślokaḥ 14

— ॐ —

असौ मया हतः शत्रुर्हनिष्ये चापरानपि ।
asau mayā hataḥ śatrurhaniṣye cāparānapi
ईश्वरोऽहमहं भोगी सिद्धोऽहं बलवान्सुखी ॥१६-१४॥
īśvaro'hamahaṁ bhogī siddho'haṁ balavānsukhī (16-14)

And this opposition has been decimated by me already and those others too I shall destroy; and I am the lord; and I am full of enjoyments; and I am powerful and successful and happy; (16.14)

—: *Word-by-Word* :—

असौ asau – that; **मया** mayā – by me; **हतः** hataḥ – has been killed; **शत्रुः** śatruḥ – enemy; **हनिष्ये** haniṣye – I shall kill; **च** ca – and; **अपरान्** aparān – others; **अपि** api – also; **ईश्वरः** īśvaraḥ – the lord; **अहम्** aham – I; **अहम्** aham – I; **भोगी** bhogī – the enjoyer; **सिद्धः** siddhaḥ – perfect; **अहम्** aham – I; **बलवान्** balavān – powerful; **सुखी** sukhī – happy.

—: *Understanding The Verse* :—

— ॐ श्रीकृष्णाय नमः ॐ —

In this verse, Shri Bhagwāna further discloses the full bloom of the āsuric disposition—a mind wholly enthralled by self-importance and illusion.

Here we witness the climactic utterance of ego, with the transient Jīva, bereft of discernment, jiving in the ballroom of delusions—proclaiming himself as the solitary wielder of power and the sole architect of his destiny! O fool, thou controlest nothing.

Puffed up with pride, intoxicated by fleeting victories, and entranced by ephemeral pleasures, the demoniac being mistakes the play of guṇas alone to be the ultimate reality of life. It is not.

— ॐ श्रीरामाय नमः ॐ —

The verse captures the voice of one who, steeped in **अविद्या** avidyā, has entirely misapprehended the nature of existence. He declares his enemies already destroyed and foretells further conquests, exalting himself as the supreme lord ईश्वर (īśvaraḥ), the exclusive enjoyer भोक्ता (bhoktā), and the paragon of strength and happiness.

The deeper irony is that this self-exaltation is but a hollow echo—a symptom of profound disconnection from the eternal Self (Ātmā) and the supreme Puruṣa.

— ॐ समुद्रसेतुबंधकर्त्रे नमः ॐ —

Thus, this verse serves as a mirror held up to the darkest recesses of human delusion, where the ego's insatiable hunger for control and supremacy culminates in a state of deep bondages, with man's own ambitions like clenched fists around his throat, his soul.

"I slew this foe, others too shall I slay," each word impales him to the world with violence unyielding—bringing only sorrows in the end.

In showing us this imagery, Bhagwāna not only illustrates the perilous path of the āsuric being but also, implicitly, invites us the साधक sādhakas to reflect upon the inner tendencies that obscure true wisdom and lead one astray from the peace of Sanātana-Dharma.

—: Key Sanskrit Terms :—

— ॐ तत सत ॐ —

Come, let us pause at the doorway of this verse, where ambition and conquest are named in words older than memory. The Sanskrit words stand before us not as foe but as mirrors—each syllable opening into the hidden hungers of human heart, warning us not to stray to the dark side.

— ॐ —

असौ मया हतः शत्रुः (Asau mayā hataḥ śatruḥ) – That enemy has been slain by me:

- असौ Asau - that (opponent/enemy).
- मया Mayā - by me (egoic agent).
- हतः Hataḥ - killed, destroyed.
- शत्रुः Śatruḥ - enemy.

The āsuric being defines identity through opposition: success is not inner fulfillment, but conquest of others.

The phrase drips with egoic triumphalism—a belief in one's supremacy, rooted in comparisons and violence.

— ॐ —

हनिष्ये च अपरानपि (Haniṣye ca aparān api) – I shall destroy others too:

- हनिष्ये Haniṣye - I shall kill.

- च ca अपि api - and also.
- अपरान Aparān - others (more enemies).

The desire to dominate expands endlessly.

Even when victory is achieved, the ego projects future threats, and plans more destruction.

Peace becomes impossible; satisfaction a horizon never reached.

— ॐ —

ईश्वरः अहम् (Īśvaraḥ aham) – I am the Lord:
- ईश्वरः Īśvaraḥ - the Supreme Ruler, God, the inner controller.
- ईश्वरः Aham - I.

The final delusion: to see oneself as the ultimate authority, independent of Braham, the śāstra, or the moral law! Wow!

This is not the beautiful self-realization exemplified by the sacred words अहं ब्रह्मास्मि (aham-braham-āsmi), but its dark mimicry—body and mind exalted, flesh and ego enthroned.

— ॐ —

अहम् भोगी (Ahaṁ bhogī) – I am the enjoyer:
- भोगी Bhogī - one who enjoys sensual pleasures.

The being sees no sacredness in life, no offering, no renunciation.

All is to be consumed, possessed, exploited.

— ॐ —

सिद्धः अहम् (Siddho'ham) – I am accomplished:
- सिद्धः Siddhaḥ can mean attained, perfected—but here, it implies worldly success, seen as self-made.

The आसुरी āsuric mind confuses material conquest with spiritual completion.

— ॐ —

बलवान् (Balavān) – I am powerful:

Physical might, political clout, intellectual dominance—these become the currency of the ego, seen as intrinsic virtue, rather than temporary attributes bestowed by karma and grace.

— ॐ —

सुखी (Sukhī) – I am happy:

Perhaps the most tragic claim!

The āsuric soul declares himself happy, but the Gītā has already revealed that such beings are riddled with चिन्ता cintā (anxieties, verse 16.11), bound by आशा पाश āśāpāśa (hopes), and enslaved to काम kāma (desires).

This happiness is illusory, fragile—dependent upon the external as it ever remains.

—: In Brief :—

— ॐ श्रीकृष्णाय नमः ॐ —

With Bhagavad Gītā 16.14 Shri Bhagwāna has unveiled the crescendo of egoic delusion—the inner voice of the āsuric jīva at its most inflated, where the self imagines itself as supreme actor, controller, enjoyer, and master.

Here, the intoxication of power बल (bala), conquest शत्रु हन (śatru-han), and pleasure भोग (bhoga) combine to form a complete severance from the true Self आत्मा (Ātmā), from humility, and from dharma.

This verse is not merely a warning against external arrogance—it is a map of inner ignorance, the soul's cry when it has forgotten its source.

— ॐ त्रिनेत्रधारिणे नमः ॐ —

This verse has unfurled the tapestry of the āsuric mindset in its full arrogance and folly. The demoniac individual, consumed by desire and wrath, revels in imagined victories and proclaims forthcoming triumphs, convinced of his absolute mastery over the world.

Such a one perceives himself as unrivaled in might and affluence, and intoxicated by these delusions, he dismisses the spiritual path as the indulgence of the weak and ignorant. Though he outwardly boasts of happiness and success, inwardly he is afflicted by ceaseless agitation—a turmoil born of insatiable cravings and the fear of loss.

— ॐ महोद्राय नमः ॐ —

Through this verse Shri Bhagwāna Krishna exposes the fragile edifice of such false pride. While these beings parade their accomplishments and suppose themselves to be beyond defeat, they are in truth ensnared by the very forces they worship—desire (kāma) and anger (krodha)—which relentlessly propel them toward spiritual ruin.

Their fleeting joys are but sparks before the engulfing darkness, for they are tethered to the transient and have severed their bond with the eternal.

— ॐ वेदवेद्याय नमः ॐ —

As we move to the subsequent verse, the Lord will deepen His exposition, unveiling the further descent of such beings—how, ensnared by countless anxieties and trapped in the web of endless desires, they spiral into deeper bondage.

The transition marks a movement from boastful proclamations to a revelation of the inner torment that inevitably afflicts those who have turned away from dharma and truth.

— ॐ तत सत ॐ —

Before we move on, let us bow in reverence to this sacred verse. Write it by hand, reflect on its meaning, chant it aloud, make it your own.

— ॐ —

असौ मया हतः शत्रुर्हनिष्ये चापरानपि ।
asau mayā hataḥ śatrurhaniṣye cāparānapi
ईश्वरोऽहमहं भोगी सिद्धोऽहं बलवान्सुखी ॥१६-१४॥
īśvaro'hamahaṁ bhogī siddho'haṁ balavānsukhī (16-14)

असौ मया हतः शत्रुर्हनिष्ये चापरानपि ।
asau mayā hataḥ śatrurhaniṣye cāparānapi
ईश्वरोऽहमहं भोगी सिद्धोऽहं बलवान्सुखी ॥१६-१४॥
īśvaro'hamahaṁ bhogī siddho'haṁ balavānsukhī (16-14)

ॐ तत्सदिति श्रीमद्भगवद्गीतासूपनिषत्सु ब्रह्मविद्यायां योगशास्त्रे श्रीकृष्णार्जुनसंवादे
om tatsaditi śrīmadbhagavadgītāsūpaniṣatsu brahmavidyāyāṁ yogaśāstre śrīkṛṣṇārjunasaṁvāde
दैवासुरसम्पद्विभागयोगो नाम षोडशोऽध्यायः श्लोकः १४
daivāsurasampadvibhāgayogo nāma ṣoḍaśo'dhyāyaḥ ślokaḥ 14

Om-Tat-Sat—Om (Braham) is the sole Reality. In the Yogic Scripture on the Science-of-Braham, the Shrimada-Bhāgvada-Gītā Upanishad, we hereby conclude Shloka 14 of the Dialogue between Shrī Krishna and Arjuna entitled Daivāsura-Sampada-Vibhāga-Yoga, Canto XVI.

<u>The Illusion of Imperial Control</u>

"I have it made—am full of toys/enjoyments," cries out their demeanor,
Aye, lofty voices indeed—but lost in the crowds.

Endless pleasures of the world are theirs to command,
But the winds of time slip from their puny frames, tiny hands.

The joy they cumulate, becomes soon the fleeting light,
Vanishing before the onslaught of the oncoming night.

Their empire of senses, stands so tall,
But the base is hollow & cracked—it *Has* to one day fall.

In their eyes, the world bends and crumbles to their will,
But the truth remains hidden, silent and still—
For in just few short years, they simply disappear—
Themselves crumpled and humbled—into dust & ash.

ॐ गीता श्लोकः १६.१५-१६ – GĪTĀ VERSE 16.15-16

ॐ श्रीमद्भगवद्गीतासूपनिषत्सु ब्रह्मविद्यायां योगशास्त्रे श्रीकृष्णार्जुनसंवादे
om śrīmadbhagavadgītāsūpaniṣatsu brahmavidyāyāṁ yogaśāstre śrīkṛṣṇārjunasaṁvāde
दैवासुरसम्पद्विभागयोगो नाम षोडशोऽध्यायः श्लोकः १५-१६
daivāsurasampadvibhāgayogo nāma ṣoḍaśo'dhyāyaḥ ślokaḥ 15-16

— ॐ —

आढ्योऽभिजनवानस्मि कोऽन्योऽस्ति सदृशो मया ।
āḍhyo'bhijanavānasmi ko'nyo'sti sadṛśo mayā
यक्ष्ये दास्यामि मोदिष्य इत्यज्ञानविमोहिताः ॥१६-१५॥
yakṣye dāsyāmi modiṣya ityajñānavimohitāḥ (16-15)

अनेकचित्तविभ्रान्ता मोहजालसमावृताः ।
anekacittavibhrāntā mohajālasamāvṛtāḥ
प्रसक्ताः कामभोगेषु पतन्ति नरकेऽशुचौ ॥१६-१६॥
prasaktāḥ kāmabhogeṣu patanti narake'śucau (16-16)

And I am princely, and I have big family, and who else here is equal to me? I shall make sacrifices and give endowments and I shall regale.'—Thus deluded by ignorance, ensnared in their web of delusions, addicted to the enjoyments of sensuous pleasures, with their minds bewildered by fanciful thoughts, these men of demoniacal dispositions, slide down into most foul hells. (16.15-16.16)

—: Word-by-Word :—

आढ्यः āḍhyaḥ – wealthy; **अभिजनवान्** abhijanavān – of noble birth; **अस्मि** asmi – I am; **कः** kaḥ – who; **अन्यः** anyaḥ – else; **अस्ति** asti – is; **सदृशः** sadṛśaḥ – equal; **मया** mayā – to me; **यक्ष्ये** yakṣye – I shall perform Yajna; **दास्यामि** dāsyāmi – I shall give (in charity); **मोदिष्ये** modiṣye – I shall rejoice; **इति** iti – thus; **अज्ञानविमोहिताः** ajñāna-vimohitāḥ – deluded by ignorance.

अनेकचित्तविभ्रान्ताः aneka-citta-vibhrāntāḥ – distracted by numerous thoughts; **मोहजालसमावृताः** moha-jāla-samāvṛtāḥ – enveloped in the net of delusion; **प्रसक्ताः** prasaktāḥ – deeply attached; **कामभोगेषु** kāma-bhogeṣu – to sensual pleasures; **पतन्ति** patanti – they fall; **नरके** narake – into hell; **अशुचौ** aśucau – impure.

—: Understanding The Verse :—

— ॐ श्रीकृष्णाय नमः ॐ —

In these verses, Shri Bhagwāna brings to culmination His penetrating portrait of the āsuric temperament, exposing with sharp clarity its inner scaffolding of pride, vanity, and delusion.

The demoniac being, intoxicated by fleeting worldly attainments, speaks in tones of boastful self-exaltation: reveling in material wealth, parading familial and social status, and imagining unmatched grandeur.

Here, the inner voice is saturated with a misplaced sense of supremacy—proclaiming their intent to perform grand sacrifices, distribute alms, and indulge in sensuous delights—not out of devotion or duty, but to hear their name echo through the hollow chambers of laurels and fame.

— ॐ श्रीरामाय नमः ॐ —

But beyond these external declarations lies a far deeper pathology. The soul ensnared in this web of self-delusion becomes increasingly estranged from dharma—becomes devoid of true spiritual anchor.

The mind, bewildered by vain imaginings and distorted aspirations, lurches aimlessly, driven by desire's tyrannical sway.

Such beings may adorn themselves with the outer symbols of virtue—charity, sacrifice, and ritual—but the spirit of surrender and true yajña is conspicuously absent.

Shri Bhagwāna thus offers a grave warning: When thought itself becomes clouded by ignorance and directed by pride and lust, the fate that awaits is not one of elevation but of degradation; and what a fall it is!—into the foulest hells, both within and in the afterlife.

These verses stand as a luminous testament to the Gītā-Dharma's central truth: that right action flows not from outward show, but from inner clarity and alignment with the eternal dharma.

— ॐ तत सत ॐ —

—: *Key Sanskrit Terms* :—

— ॐ तत सत ॐ —

What is being talked about in the verse is of the Dark side, but let us still sit at its threshold—not necessarily as the pilgrims but as visitors of the unseen; and let us receive the Sanskrit offerings—for they come straight from the very lips of the Divine, and are like incense at the altar of Truth that keeps the stench away.

Let us pray to Krishna that we never stray away from the Way of Gītā-Dharma—never allow the stench of āsurī pravritti to ever come our way, enter our life.

— ॐ श्रीकृष्णाय नमः ॐ —

Verse 16.15

Here we listen as the verse gathers its sounds into a mask of pride and wealth. The Sanskrit does not accuse, it simply reveals—like a lamp tilted so shadows fall away, leaving the hollow shapes exposed.

आढ्यः अभिजनवान् अस्मि (Āḍhyaḥ abhijanavān asmi) – I am wealthy and of noble birth:

- आढ्यः Āḍhyaḥ - rich, possessing great material wealth.
- अभिजनवान् Abhijanavān - high-born, of noble lineage.

These are marks of laukika māna—worldly pride. The soul identifies not with the Self, but with external attributes: wealth, caste, ancestry—as if they confer intrinsic worth.

— ॐ —

कः अन्यः अस्ति सदृशः मया (Kaḥ anyaḥ asti sadṛśaḥ mayā) – Who else is equal to me?

Lo, this is the ego's peak: solipsism, the inability to perceive any reality or value beyond one's body and mind.

This rhetorical question shows utter arrogance, a mind that sees itself as unmatched, sovereign, supreme.

— ॐ —

यक्ष्ये (Yakṣye) – I shall sacrifice (to the gods)

This is religion corrupted by pride. The āsuric soul may still perform ritual (yajña), but it is not for surrender or purification, only for personal gain or display.

— ॐ —

दास्यामि (Dāsyāmi) – I will give / donate

Even दान dāna (charity), a noble act, is co-opted by ego. The gift is not an offering, but a tool of self-aggrandizement.

— ॐ —

मोदिष्ये (Modiṣye) – I will rejoice / enjoy

The final goal: indulgence.

This is not the bliss of Self-realization आनन्द (ānanda)—far from it—but fleeting delight rooted in the senses.

It is the momentary सुख sukha, of a being unmindful of his true nature—of himself being bliss-embodied: the Ātmā, whence all bliss emerges.

— ॐ —

अज्ञानविमोहिताः (Ajñāna-vimohitāḥ) – Deluded by ignorance

The root cause: अज्ञान ajñāna, ignorance of the Self.
विमोहिताः Vimohitaḥ means utterly bewildered.
This is not simply lacking sanātana knowledge, but actively misled, wrapped in the spell of illusion (mohā).

— ॐ श्रीकृष्णाय नमः ॐ —

Verse 16.16

This śloka rises and falls like a tide—the Sanskrit syllables swelling and receding as desire builds its own storm.
But let us follow the rhythm inward. The true purpose of the verse is to remind us, to warn us—for us to stay wary—of the deep undertow that pulls the jiva away and drowns him.

— ॐ —

अनेकचित्तविभ्रान्ताः (Aneka-citta-vibhrāntāḥ) – Confused by countless thoughts:
- अनेक Aneka - countless, many.
- चित्त Citta - mind, thought.
- विभ्रान्ताः Vibhrāntaḥ - unsteady, deluded, scattered.

The mind is fragmented, racing in many directions.
Desires, fears, plans, comparisons—all pull the jiva in varied directions.
There is no center. Consequently there is no peace for him—he who strays away from Sanātana-Dharma.

— ॐ —

मोहजालसमावृताः (Moha-jāla-samāvṛtāḥ) – Ensnared in the net of delusion:
- मोह Moha - illusion, spiritual blindness.
- जाल Jāla - net, snare.
- समावृताः Samāvṛtāḥ - completely enveloped.

These beings are not lightly misled, but ensnared, like fish caught in a net woven of false beliefs, egoic thoughts, and sensual desires.
They cannot see the reality of existence.

— ॐ —

प्रसक्ताः कामभोगेषु (Prasaktāḥ kāma-bhogeṣu) – Attached to sensual pleasures:
- प्रसक्ताः Prasaktaḥ - deeply attached, clinging.
- कामभोगेषु Kāma-bhogeṣu - objects of pleasure born from desire.

Their devotion is to Indulgences, not the Divine. Their clinging becomes their bondage—each pleasure a link in the chain binding them.

— ॐ —

पतन्ति नरके अशुचौ (Patanti narake aśucau) – They fall into hells, most foul:

- पतन्ति Patanti - they fall, descend.
- नरक Naraka - hell—it is not merely a place, but it is a state of being, a realm of suffering.
- अशुचौ Aśucau - impure, defiled, unholy.

The inevitable result of unrestrained desire, delusion, and ego is a fall into darkness—into suffering, into further rebirths, into a life disconnected from purity and the Self.

—: *In Brief* :—

— ॐ श्रीकृष्णाय नमः ॐ —

These two verses—Bhagavad Gītā 16.15–16—form a profound culmination of Bhagwāna's revelation of the āsuric inner world.

Here, Bhagwāna Shri Krishna, out Lord Divine does not merely describe evil actions or false beliefs, but offers a vivid, almost tragic monologue of the deluded soul—inflated by pride, obsessed with pleasure, and caught in a dazzling web of self-deception.

Together, these verses are a luminous warning:
- when the ego becomes the deity,
- when kāma (desire) and mohā (delusion) become guiding lights,

—then the soul is pulled steadily away from dharma, from purity, from Self-knowledge—ultimately into blinding darkness from where one is able to extricate himself out only with great effort, suffering through unnumbered births.

— ॐ श्रीरामाय नमः ॐ —

Alas! Pride wears a mask until it eats into the face beneath.

Drunk on wealth, swollen with vanity, man forgets himself—until the mask shatters, revealing nothing but a within emptiness.

Desire breeds desire, delusion multiplies upon itself.
Like waves without rest they crash, dragging the soul downward into darker waters, until only ruin remains.

— ॐ चतुर्भुजाय नमः ॐ —

These verses expose the hollowness and tragic folly of the demoniac nature.

Such individuals, bloated with self-conceit, trumpet their wealth, their lineage, their multitude of followers, and imagine themselves unparalleled in status and grandeur.

Their boast to undertake sacrifices and distribute charity is not born of any true sacrificial spirit, but springs from a craving for recognition, a thirst for outward applause.

Even their so-called religious acts are tainted by selfishness, a mere performance designed to inscribe their names upon monuments of fleeting glory.

— ॐ श्रीकृष्णगोविंदाय नमः ॐ —

The doom that shadows such prideful delusion is grim indeed. The Lord reveals that these souls, ensnared by the twin serpents of desire and ignorance, spiral inexorably toward infernal destinies.

Their mind, saturated with fancies and distorted visions, is unable to grasp the higher truth, and thus they wallow in inner turmoil even as they chase after pleasures.

The 'hells' they fall into are not merely the real realms of punishment after death but begin even in this very life, as their hearts are consumed by the fires of dissatisfaction, rivalry, and unrest.

In essence, Shri Bhagwāna underscores a profound spiritual law: that it is not merely external actions but the very texture of one's thoughts and intentions that shape destiny.

The seeds of downfall are sown in the soil of inner corruption long before they bear fruit outwardly—in this life and the afterlife.

— ॐ यज्वने नमः ॐ —

Make no mistake O mortal—there ***are*** realms beyond this earthly realms—the realms of heavens and hells; and there the soul goes after death—to reap the fruits of karmas of this earthly life – before he takes rebirth again in a physical body—that of a ordinary creature or as a human creature— to continue his endless sorrowful journey of life.

So make good use of this human birth we have this time around, O friend, and taking to the path of Gītā-Dharma let’s strive to get out of this dateless sorrowful cycle of transmigration.

— ॐ अनन्तवीर्याय नमः ॐ —

As we proceed further, we find the Lord unmasking the deeper malaise of the demoniac mind—how, driven by insatiable desires and shackled by illusion, such beings engage in perverse ritualism and distorted sacrifices, further binding themselves to saṁsāra's wheel of suffering.

Thus, the transition from mere boasting to the nature of their actual sacrificial acts marks a deepening of the discourse in the next verse.

— ॐ तत सत ॐ —

Before we move on, let us bow in reverence to this sacred verse—a timeless beacon of wisdom guiding seekers for ages. Write it by hand, reflect on its meaning, and chant it aloud, for these sounds alone carry the authenticity of that era. The world may have changed but the living vibration of these Sanskrit sounds still remain as original as they were when Bhagwān Shri Krishna Himself walked the earth and imparted these teachings.

— ॐ —

आढ्योऽभिजनवानस्मि कोऽन्योऽस्ति सदृशो मया ।
ādhyo'bhijanavānasmi ko'nyo'sti sadṛśo mayā
यक्ष्ये दास्यामि मोदिष्य इत्यज्ञानविमोहिताः ॥ १६-१५ ॥
yakṣye dāsyāmi modiṣya ityajñānavimohitāḥ (16-15)
अनेकचित्तविभ्रान्ता मोहजालसमावृताः ।
anekacittavibhrāntā mohajālasamāvṛtāḥ
प्रसक्ताः कामभोगेषु पतन्ति नरकेऽशुचौ ॥ १६-१६ ॥
prasaktāḥ kāmabhogeṣu patanti narake'śucau (16-16)

— ॐ —

आढ्योऽभिजनवानस्मि कोऽन्योऽस्ति सदृशो मया ।
ādhyo'bhijanavānasmi ko'nyo'sti sadṛśo mayā
यक्ष्ये दास्यामि मोदिष्य इत्यज्ञानविमोहिताः ॥ १६-१५ ॥
yakṣye dāsyāmi modiṣya ityajñānavimohitāḥ (16-15)
अनेकचित्तविभ्रान्ता मोहजालसमावृताः ।
anekacittavibhrāntā mohajālasamāvṛtāḥ
प्रसक्ताः कामभोगेषु पतन्ति नरकेऽशुचौ ॥ १६-१६ ॥
prasaktāḥ kāmabhogeṣu patanti narake'śucau (16-16)

ॐ तत्सदिति श्रीमद्भगवद्गीतासूपनिषत्सु ब्रह्मविद्यायां योगशास्त्रे श्रीकृष्णार्जुनसंवादे
om tatsaditi śrīmadbhagavadgītāsūpaniṣatsu brahmavidyāyāṁ yogaśāstre śrīkṛṣṇārjunasaṁvāde
दैवासुरसम्पद्विभागयोगो नाम षोडशोऽध्यायः श्लोकः १५-१६
daivāsurasampadvibhāgayogo nāma ṣoḍaśo'dhyāyaḥ ślokaḥ 15-16

Om-Tat-Sat—Om (Braham) is the sole Reality. In the Yogic Scripture on the Science-of-Braham, the Shrimada-Bhāgvada-Gītā Upanishad, we hereby conclude Shloka 15-16 of the Dialogue between Shrī Krishna and Arjuna entitled Daivāsura-Sampada-Vibhāga-Yoga, Canto XVI.

ॐ गीता श्लोकः १६.१७-१८ – Gītā Verse 16.17-18

ॐ श्रीमद्भगवद्गीतासूपनिषत्सु ब्रह्मविद्यायां योगशास्त्रे श्रीकृष्णार्जुनसंवादे
om śrīmadbhagavadgītāsūpaniṣatsu brahmavidyāyāṁ yogaśāstre śrīkṛṣṇārjunasaṁvāde
दैवासुरसम्पद्विभागयोगो नाम षोडशोऽध्यायः श्लोकः १७-१८
daivāsurasampadvibhāgayogo nāma ṣoḍaśo'dhyāyaḥ ślokaḥ 17-18

— ॐ —

आत्मसम्भाविताः स्तब्धा धनमानमदान्विताः ।
ātmasambhāvitāḥ stabdhā dhanamānamadānvitāḥ
यजन्ते नामयज्ञैस्ते दम्भेनाविधिपूर्वकम् ॥१६-१७॥
yajante nāmayajñaiste dambhenāvidhipūrvakam (16-17)

अहङ्कारं बलं दर्पं कामं क्रोधं च संश्रिताः ।
ahaṅkāraṁ balaṁ darpaṁ kāmaṁ krodhaṁ ca saṁśritāḥ
मामात्मपरदेहेषु प्रद्विषन्तोऽभ्यसूयकाः ॥१६-१८॥
māmātmaparadeheṣu pradviṣanto'bhyasūyakāḥ (16-18)

Arrogant, vainglorious, intoxicated with wealth, haughty and ostentatious, performing sacrifices (Yajna) only in name, discarding the prescribed rites; given over to conceit, brute power, insolence, lust, anger—they perform Karmas in contempt of Me, hateful of the very soul which abides within them and others. (16.17-16.18)

—: Word-by-Word :—

आत्मसम्भाविताः ātma-sambhāvitāḥ – self-conceited; **स्तब्धाः** stabdhāḥ – arrogant; **धनमानमदान्विताः** dhana-māna-madānvitāḥ – filled with wealth, pride, and arrogance; **यजन्ते** yajante – they perform Yajna; **नामयज्ञैः** nāma-yajñaiḥ – in name only; **ते** te – they; **दम्भेन** dambhena – out of hypocrisy; **अविधिपूर्वकम्** avidhi-pūrvakam – without following prescribed rules.

अहङ्कारम् ahaṅkāram – ego; **बलम्** balam – strength; **दर्पम्** darpam – arrogance; **कामम्** kāmam – desire; **क्रोधम्** krodham – anger; **च** ca – and; **संश्रिताः** saṁśritāḥ – resorting to; **माम्** mām – Me; **आत्मपरदेहेषु** ātma-para-deheṣu – in their own and others' bodies; **प्रद्विषन्तः** pradviṣantaḥ – hating; **अभ्यसूयकाः** abhyasūyakāḥ – envious.

—: Understanding The Verse :—

— ॐ श्रीकृष्णाय नमः ॐ —

In these twin verses, Shri Bhagwāna deepens His portrayal of the āsuric disposition, now laying bare not merely the outward conduct but the very inner corrosion that fuels it.

The vision is grim yet precise: the demoniac beings, swollen with pride and intoxicated by the illusion of power and wealth, enact sacrifices and virtuous deeds, but these are but empty shells—mere exhibitions performed for public acclaim, bereft of true devotion or scriptural fidelity.

— ॐ श्रीरामाय नमः ॐ —

Here, the Lord illuminates the essence of false religiosity—a condition where outer forms of yajña are meticulously performed, but the sanctity of heart and surrender of ego are absent.

The attitude of such beings is steeped in egotism (ahaṅkāra), brute force (bala), insolence (darpā), and the fires of lust and anger (kāma-krodha).

These vices do not merely taint their actions; they culminate in a profound hatred—hatred not only of others but, in truth, of the Divine Presence, both within and without, that animates all beings. This is the pinnacle of their fall: a blindness so complete that they despise the very spark of Divinity that constitutes their own essence.

— ॐ सर्वतीर्थमयाय नमः ॐ —

These verses form a grave exposition of spiritual decay—where even acts outwardly noble are corrupted from within, and serve only to deepen the bondage of the soul.

They also remind the sincere seeker that true yajña is not an outward show but an inward surrender, where humility, reverence, and scriptural alignment sanctify every offering made.

—: Key Sanskrit Terms :—

— ॐ तत सत ॐ —

So we examine the verse. We pause at one word, then another—not to extract but to dwell. To wait until the silence around the syllables begins to whisper back the truths of human life.

— ॐ श्रीकृष्णाय नमः ॐ —

Verse 16.17

We step into this verse as one enters a shrine thick with incense. The Sanskrit rises like smoke, curling around conceit and false devotion—not condemning, only unveiling what worship becomes when the heart has strayed.

— ॐ —

आत्मसम्भाविताः (ātmasambhāvitāḥ)

This compound word signifies those who hold a self-conferred high opinion of themselves. आत्म "Ātma" means self (not आत्मा Ātmā, the Self), and सम्भाविताः "sambhāvita" means esteemed or honored.

Here, it denotes individuals who, without the sanction of true merit or scriptural validation, imagine themselves as great and virtuous, swelling with pride born not of wisdom but of self-conceit.

— ॐ —

स्तब्धाः (stabdhāḥ)

Literally, "rigid" or "stiffened," this word points to their inflexibility, arrogance, and closed-heartedness.

A स्तब्ध stabdha individual is unyielding, not in dharma but in egotism, frozen in false self-importance and devoid of humility—like one stunned in the head.

— ॐ —

धनमानमदान्विताः (dhanamānamadānvitāḥ)

This triad is crucial:

- धन Dhana – wealth,
- मान Māna – prestige or worldly honor,
- मद Mada – intoxication or pride.

The compound shows how wealth leads to the delusion of superiority मान (māna), which then fosters intoxicated pride मद (mada), binding the soul deeper into संसार saṁsāra through false identification.

— ॐ —

यजन्ते नाम-यज्ञैः (yajante nāma-yajñaiḥ)

They perform यज्ञ yajñas (sacrificial rites), but these are mere नाम मात्र nāma-mātra, merely in name; yajñas – only as an outer show.

There is no true spirit of surrender श्रद्धा (śraddhā), no sanctity of offering ईश्वरार्पण (īśvarārpaṇa). The external act is present, but the internal alignment with dharma is absent.

— ॐ —

दम्भेन (dambhena)

This is the false show of religiosity – hypocrisy.

दम्भ Dambha is ostentation born of ego, where one performs religious rites for display rather than devotion—thus tainting the sacred with the profanity of their vanity.

— ॐ —

अविधिपूर्वकम् (avidhi-pūrvakam)

विधि Vidhi refers to prescribed method or scriptural ordinance.

अविधिपूर्वकम् Avidhipūrvakam signifies that these sacrifices are undertaken without adherence to scriptural injunctions – a reflection of egoistic arbitrariness rather than obedience to divine law.

— ॐ श्रीकृष्णाय नमः ॐ —

Verse 16.18

Here the verse speaks with the gravity of iron doors closing. The Sanskrit syllables echo like chains, not to frighten us but to make us feel the weight of cruelty, the finality of hatred set in motion.

— ॐ —

अहङ्कारम् (ahaṅkāraṁ)

The great deluder, ego. अहङ्कार Ahaṅkāra is the misidentification of the Self with the body-mind complex. It is the seed from which all bondage arises.

In this context, it is the force that impels one to see oneself as the doer and enjoyer, severing the vision of the Self as Braham.

— ॐ —

बलं, दर्पं (balaṁ, darpaṁ)

बल Bala is brute strength, divorced from dharma.

दर्प Darpa is haughtiness – the pride that refuses to bow before Truth. Both are tamasic in nature, reinforcing the ego's fortress.

— ॐ —

कामं, क्रोधं (kāmaṁ, krodhaṁ): Desire and anger, arising from the unfulfilled ego.

काम Kāma arises from rajas and, when obstructed, turns into क्रोध krodha. These are destructive flames that consume spiritual discernment विवेक (viveka).

— ॐ —

माम आत्मपरदेहेषु प्रद्विषन्तः (mām ātma-paradeheṣu pradviṣantaḥ)

This is a subtle and poignant phrase. The Lord declares that such persons despise Him माम (mām) who resides equally in आत्म ātma (their own Self) and in पर-देह para-deha (others' bodies).

It reflects their aversion not merely toward God in temple or form, but toward the immanent Reality pervading all beings.

This is the highest form of abhyasūyā – envy or fault-finding with the Supreme Himself!

—: In Brief :—

— ॐ श्रीकृष्णाय नमः ॐ —

Self-conceit rises like incense spoiled in its own smoke—sweetness turned bitter, offering turned false.

Hypocrisy and arrogance cloud the heart of the āsurics—until their worship uprises only as distortion—pungent and empty.

Hate and cruelty forge their own fetters.

Like iron chains clanging shut, the lowest of men bind themselves fast—cast far from grace, each word of their life falling heavy, final.

— ॐ श्रीरामाय नमः ॐ —

In summing up these verses, Shri Bhagwāna reveals that those of demoniac nature, gripped by pride and deep-seated jealousy, enact yajñas not from faith or reverence, but merely to assert their own superiority.

Such persons seek not communion with the Divine but the hollow applause of the world. They inwardly scoff at the efficacy of dharma and the unseen fruits of righteous action, dismissing them as naïve beliefs.

Thus, when others engage in acts of virtue, these demoniac beings project their own shallow motives onto them, convinced that all sacrifice is mere performance, as empty as their own.

— ॐ धनुर्धराय नमः ॐ —

Their entire existence is a theater of arrogance: they consider themselves paragons of wisdom and virtue, looking down upon others as ignorant and insignificant.

Cloaked in the illusion of their own grandeur, they become impervious to true understanding, trapped in a fortress of their own making.

Their obstinacy hardens into a creed, and because their inner life is one of unrest and turmoil, they instinctively sow discord and suffering wherever they go.

To them, virtue in others is invisible, for their own vision is clouded by self-conceit; they see only flaws in others, while imagining themselves to be the sole custodians of righteousness.

In hating and harming others, these beings unknowingly wage war upon the Supreme Himself, for He abides in all beings as the indwelling Self (Ātmā).

Every act of antagonism toward another is, in truth, an act of enmity toward the Divine dwelling both in others and within one's own heart.

— ॐ सर्वपापहराय नमः ॐ —

Having now thoroughly unveiled the inner machinery of the demoniac disposition—from its thoughts to its actions—the Lord prepares to reveal the inevitable destiny that awaits such beings.

In the subsequent verses, He spells out their evil fate with unflinching clarity, drawing the ultimate contrast between the path of darkness and the path of light—that the wise may recoil from such vice and cling all the more firmly to truth, to Sanātana-Dharma—taking to the Way of Gītā-Dharma.

— ॐ तत सत ॐ —

Before we move on, let us bow in reverence to this sacred verse—a timeless beacon of wisdom guiding seekers for ages. Write it by hand, reflect on its meaning, and chant it aloud, for these sounds alone carry the authenticity of that era. The world may have changed but the living vibration of these Sanskrit sounds still remain as original as they were when Bhagwān Shri Krishna Himself walked the earth and imparted these teachings.

— ॐ —

आत्मसम्भाविताः स्तब्धा धनमानमदान्विताः ।
ātmasambhāvitāḥ stabdhā dhanamānamadānvitāḥ
यजन्ते नामयज्ञैस्ते दम्भेनाविधिपूर्वकम् ॥ १६-१७॥
yajante nāmayajñaiste dambhenāvidhipūrvakam (16-17)
अहङ्कारं बलं दर्पं कामं क्रोधं च संश्रिताः ।
ahaṅkāraṁ balaṁ darpaṁ kāmaṁ krodhaṁ ca saṁśritāḥ
मामात्मपरदेहेषु प्रद्विषन्तोऽभ्यसूयकाः ॥ १६-१८॥
māmātmaparadeheṣu pradviṣanto'bhyasūyakāḥ (16-18)

— ॐ —

आत्मसम्भाविताः स्तब्धा धनमानमदान्विताः ।
ātmasambhāvitāḥ stabdhā dhanamānamadānvitāḥ
यजन्ते नामयज्ञैस्ते दम्भेनाविधिपूर्वकम् ॥ १६-१७॥
yajante nāmayajñaiste dambhenāvidhipūrvakam (16-17)
अहङ्कारं बलं दर्पं कामं क्रोधं च संश्रिताः ।
ahaṅkāraṁ balaṁ darpaṁ kāmaṁ krodhaṁ ca saṁśritāḥ
मामात्मपरदेहेषु प्रद्विषन्तोऽभ्यसूयकाः ॥ १६-१८॥
māmātmaparadeheṣu pradviṣanto'bhyasūyakāḥ (16-18)

ॐ तत्सदिति श्रीमद्भगवद्गीतासूपनिषत्सु ब्रह्मविद्यायां योगशास्त्रे श्रीकृष्णार्जुनसंवादे
om tatsaditi śrīmadbhagavadgītāsūpaniṣatsu brahmavidyāyāṁ yogaśāstre śrīkṛṣṇārjunasaṁvāde
दैवासुरसम्पद्विभागयोगो नाम षोडशोऽध्यायः श्लोकः १७-१८
daivāsurasampadvibhāgayogo nāma ṣoḍaśo'dhyāyaḥ ślokaḥ 17-18

Om-Tat-Sat—Om (Braham) is the sole Reality. In the Yogic Scripture on the Science-of-Braham, the Shrimada-Bhāgvada-Gītā Upanishad, we hereby conclude Shloka 17-18 of the Dialogue between Shrī Krishna and Arjuna entitled Daivāsura-Sampada-Vibhāga-Yoga, Canto XVI.

"I try to Drape me in Glory,"

"I give handouts. I perform charities, pujas, yajnas."
But the fire remains cold,
And the altar echoes only with self-praise.
The mantras rise—
But never reach the ear of the Infinite.

He follows Vidhi-hinam विधि हीनं – The Unanchored Path

No scriptures, No compass.
Only the little self, the ego, as his guide.
Carving his own way through the jungle of infinite desires,
He rewrites the sacred in the ink of arrogance.

He is the High-Priest of Pride

His worth is his wealth.
His lineage?—The lamp of glory shining on the lines of his face.
He bows not in temples—but before mirrors.
His yajña is a performance for an audience of three: "I, Me, Myself".

He makes the Sounds of Mantras—

But only his name and desires ring inside the chants.
Even silence feels crowded and leaves—
In the presence of his all mighty Importance.

Devoid of Dharma's might.

His deeds are performed blankly, inanely—
Mechanical hands, moored to a hollow head.
He does not necessarily choose the dark—
Stunned and zombie like,
He has simply lost all regard for Light.

He lives without a Star—nor seeks the inward Light.

Raised on the modern system of Malichs, Tethered to Untruth,
Unknown to Sanâtana ways, Unmoored from rite and rules,
Life after life, he stays drifting endlessly—
on the roiling waves of this evanescent life.

ॐ गीता श्लोकः १६.१९ – Gītā Verse 16.19

ॐ श्रीमद्भगवद्गीतासूपनिषत्सु ब्रह्मविद्यायां योगशास्त्रे श्रीकृष्णार्जुनसंवादे
om śrīmadbhagavadgītāsūpaniṣatsu brahmavidyāyāṁ yogaśāstre śrīkṛṣṇārjunasaṁvāde
दैवासुरसम्पद्विभागयोगो नाम षोडशोऽध्यायः श्लोकः १९
daivāsurasampadvibhāgayogo nāma ṣoḍaśo'dhyāyaḥ ślokaḥ 19

— ॐ —

तानहं द्विषतः क्रूरान्संसारेषु नराधमान् ।
tānahaṁ dviṣataḥ krūrānsaṁsāreṣu narādhamān
क्षिपाम्यजस्रमशुभानासुरीष्वेव योनिषु ॥१६-१९॥
kṣipāmyajasramaśubhānāsurīṣveva yoniṣu (16-19)

Such cruel haters—these sinful and most degraded of humans—them I ever cast into the wombs of demoniacal species of the world, to revolve in an unremitting transmigratory cycle. (16.19)

—: Word-by-Word :—

तान् tān – those; **अहम्** aham – I; **द्विषतः** dviṣataḥ – hateful; **क्रूरान्** krūrān – cruel; **संसारेषु** saṁsāreṣu – in the cycle of worldly existence; **नराधमान्** narādhamān – the vilest among men; **क्षिपामि** kṣipāmi – cast; **अजस्रम्** ajasram – perpetually; **अशुभान्** aśubhān – the inauspicious ones; **आसुरीषु** āsurīṣu – into demoniac; **एव** eva – indeed; **योनिषु** yoniṣu – wombs.

—: Understanding The Verse :—

— ॐ श्रीकृष्णाय नमः ॐ —

This verse, Bhagavad Gītā 16.19, resounds with one of the most formidable pronouncements of Divine justice and cosmic order.

Having unveiled through preceding verses the dark tapestry of the āsuric disposition—the pride, hatred, cruelty, and disdain for the Divine—Shri Bhagwāna now discloses the eventual karmic consequence that awaits such souls. The language is direct and unflinching, underscoring the gravity of sinfulness that has become entrenched.

— ॐ श्रीरामाय नमः ॐ —

Here, the Lord describes how those given over to cruelty (krūra), steeped in hatred (dveṣa), and embodying the basest human tendencies (narādhamāḥ), are consigned to repeated births within the wombs of demoniacal species.

This cycle is not merely a punishment but a reflection of the immutable law of karma, wherein beings are drawn to environments and forms of existence that mirror their inner tendencies.

The term आसुरीषु योनिषु 'āsurīṣu yonīṣu' signifies not only literal births in lower species but also symbolizes a state of existence steeped in ignorance, violence, and spiritual blindness.

— ॐ मेघश्यामाय नमः ॐ —

Crucially, the Lord's casting of such beings is not borne of wrath or revenge; rather, it is a facet of Divine compassion and cosmic justice, designed to chasten, refine, and, in the long arc of transmigration, offer the potential for eventual upliftment.

Like a wise teacher who disciplines not out of anger but out of love, the Divine steers even the most fallen souls toward the path of purification, albeit through rigorous and painful means.

Thus, this verse stands as both a solemn warning and a hidden assurance: that while the wheels of justice turn unfailingly, the ultimate aim is always the soul's return to his true nature: the radiant Self, the Ātmā.

This śloka burns like a fire that leaps skyward.
Its Sanskrit words crackle and flare, casting light on the truth of destiny repeated—each sound reminding us that what we choose, that only we become again and again.

—: Key Sanskrit Terms :—

— ॐ तत सत ॐ —

Now let us allow the Sanskrit to speak in its own time, in its own way—like wind through trees or waves on shore—saying only what the soul is ready to hear.

— ॐ —

तान् अहं द्विषतः (tān ahaṁ dviṣataḥ)
- तान् Tān – "those" (referring to individuals previously described in verses 16.17–18).
- द्विषतः Dviṣataḥ – from the root द्विष dviṣ, "to hate."
These are not just those who disbelieve or err in understanding, but those whose hearts are actively antagonistic toward the Divine, toward Sanātana-Dharma, toward the Self residing in all beings.
The word evokes a malignant will, not mere ignorance.

— ॐ —

क्रूरान् (krūrān): क्रूर Krūra refers to cruelty—violent, pitiless behavior.
It implies a tamasic and unrefined disposition, where compassion दया (dayā) is absent, and selfish desire rules. Such persons violate—do अहिंसा ahimsā, not merely in act, but in thought and intent.

— ॐ —

संसारेषु नराधमान् (saṁsāreṣu narādhamān)

- संसार Saṁsāra – the perpetual cycle of birth, death, and rebirth, governed by karma and desire.

- नराधमान् Narādhamān – "the vilest among men." A composite of nara नर (man) and अधम adhamāḥ (the lowest).

These are no mere ordinary sinners but those who actively degrade the human birth—which birth is esteemed and prized in Sanātana-Dharma as a unique opportunity for gaining emancipation, getting the hell out of this transmigratory suffering -- gyrating madly in the world of heavens, earths and hells.

— ॐ —

क्षिपामि (kṣipāmi): A powerful verb meaning "I hurl" or "I cast."
It is not a passive allowance but an active and deliberate act of Divine governance—not in malice, but in strict adherence to cosmic justice (ऋत ṛta).

The Lord does not punish whimsically but redirects the soul according to its inner tendencies वासना (vāsanās).

— ॐ —

अजिस्त्रम् (ajasram): Meaning "unceasingly" or "without interruption."
It signifies the cyclical persistence of such a soul's bondage, reflecting the inertia of deeply embedded āsuric dispositions, requiring many births for eventual correction or exhaustion of karmic momentum.

— ॐ —

अशुभान् (aśubhān): That which is impure, inauspicious, unholy.
These are beings devoid of शुभ संस्कार śubha-samskāras—good impressions formed by righteous thoughts and deeds.

Their mental fabric is woven with threads of adharma—of tamas and rajas.

— ॐ —

आसुरीषु एव योनिषु (āsurīṣu eva yoniṣu)

- आसुरीषु योनिषु Āsurīṣu yoniṣu – wombs or birth-conditions of demoniacal nature.

- योनि Yoni does not merely refer to biological species but includes states of consciousness, tendencies, and existential conditions aligned with āsuric qualities—pride, delusion, cruelty, and hatred.

In this context, being cast into "demonic wombs" means rebirths suited to reinforce and play out these dark tendencies until they are eventually exhausted or transformed.

—: *In Brief* :—

— ॐ श्रीकृष्णाय नमः ॐ —

Fury leaps like a fire unquenched. Again and again the soul is hurled into burning wombs of darkness—each destiny seared with inexorable flame.

In this grave pronouncement, Shri Bhagwāna makes it clear that those whose hearts are hardened by cruelty, arrogance, and hatred are propelled, by their own nature, into repeated births among demoniac beings.

— ॐ श्रीरामाय नमः ॐ —

The term आसुरी योनि 'āsurī yonī' evokes a vivid picture: wombs of creatures marked by instinct, darkness, ferocity —hyenas, canines, scorpions and the like.

Yet the Lord's action is not one of spite but of divine stewardship.
As a mother disciplines her wayward child for his ultimate good, so too does the Lord consign these souls to conditions that reflect their inner states, with the aim of purifying them through the fires of experience.

— ॐ चित्रकूट समाश्रयाय नमः ॐ —

The Lord, being the Supreme Well-wisher of all beings (sarva-bhūta-hite rataḥ), acts always out of compassion, even when the means appear stern.

These births are, in truth, remedial stations along the soul's arduous journey toward eventual redemption.
No pain. No gain.
Jiva is given that pain so that he never strays that painful way again.

While worldly friends and kinsmen may indulge their beloveds, thereby deepening their entanglement in saṁsāra, the Lord's discipline serves a higher purpose: to cleanse the soul of its encrusted sins and, in due course, restore it to the path of dharma.

— ॐ चतुर्भुजाय नमः ॐ —

Come O asura, were it not for the crust of ignorance built thick upon thy soul—you would verily be God.

And our great Rishis have been proclaiming for ages: तत् त्वम् असि tat-tvam-asi: That thou art, verily God.

Give thyself a chance, O mortal. Get out of this Asuric mindset even now; otherwise hell and great suffering and pain await thee—and surely thou shalt learn at then -- while lamenting and wringing hands at opportunities wasted in this precious human birth.

Come, be that wise child who mends himself before the rod of chastisement falls.

— ॐ वैदेहीप्रियाय नमः ॐ —

The Gītā has already established that the root of all such degradation lies in the pelage of ignorance and debris clinging thick upon the soul—unchecked desires (kāma) and its progeny: greed, anger, and violence.

As desire intensifies, man resorts to deceit, injustice, and cruelty, thereby darkening his karmic ledger and sealing his fate in lower realms of existence.

Ah, this is a vicious circle most terrible.

— ॐ द्वारकानायकाय नमः ॐ —

Having thus revealed the inexorable consequence of demoniac tendencies, Shri Bhagwāna, in the following verse, will unveil the ultimate destiny that awaits these souls after repeated degradation—a descent into the darkest realms of existence, from which ascent becomes exceedingly difficult. The transition further deepens our understanding of karma's relentless precision and the need for vigilant self-purification.

— ॐ तत सत ॐ —

Before we move on, let us bow in reverence to this sacred verse—a timeless beacon of wisdom guiding seekers for ages. Write it by hand, reflect on its meaning, and chant it aloud, for these sounds alone carry the authenticity of that era. The world may have changed but the living vibration of these Sanskrit sounds still remain as original as they were when Bhagwān Shri Krishna Himself walked the earth and imparted these teachings.

— ॐ —

तानहं द्विषतः क्रूरान्संसारेषु नराधमान् ।
tānahaṁ dviṣataḥ krūrānsaṁsāreṣu narādhamān
क्षिपाम्यजस्रमशुभानासुरीष्वेव योनिषु ॥ १६-१९ ॥
kṣipāmyajasramaśubhānāsurīṣveva yoniṣu (16-19)

—ॐ—

तानहं द्विषतः क्रूरान्संसारेषु नराधमान् ।
tānahaṁ dviṣataḥ krūrānsaṁsāreṣu narādhamān
क्षिपाम्यजस्रमशुभानासुरीष्वेव योनिषु ॥ १६-१९ ॥
kṣipāmyajasramaśubhānāsurīṣveva yoniṣu (16-19)

ॐ तत्सदिति श्रीमद्भगवद्गीतासूपनिषत्सु ब्रह्मविद्यायां योगशास्त्रे श्रीकृष्णार्जुनसंवादे
om tatsaditi śrīmadbhagavadgītāsūpaniṣatsu brahmavidyāyāṁ yogaśāstre śrīkṛṣṇārjunasaṁvāde
दैवासुरसम्पद्विभागयोगो नाम षोडशोऽध्यायः श्लोकः १९
daivāsurasampadvibhāgayogo nāma ṣoḍaśo'dhyāyaḥ ślokaḥ 19

Om-Tat-Sat—Om (Braham) is the sole Reality. In the Yogic Scripture on the Science-of-Braham, the Shrimada-Bhāgvada-Gītā Upanishad, we hereby conclude Shloka 19 of the Dialogue between Shrī Krishna and Arjuna entitled Daivāsura-Sampada-Vibhāga-Yoga, Canto XVI.

Kroorah क्रूर – The Hardened Heart
His hand is heavy.
His smile quite sharp,
Not by mistake, but by design—
that's the modern day asura's new found art.
He hates what reminds him of what he threw away, lost—
The Divinity he himself once was.

Narâdhamân नराधमान् – His Fall Is Chosen
Not born low—but himself made low,
By choices whispered in the language of ego.
Born in a Sanâtani home, raised with scripture in his hand—
the Macullû chose instead, to ape the West, and become a brutish ape.

He'll be Cast Down To Wear the Skin of Lowly Creatures after Death
Not by wrath, but by reflection,
Bhagwāna sends him where his heart will well resonate next.
A birth to match the karmas and mindset he cultivated all his life.

The Ape is Reborn through Darkened Wombs: आसुरी योनि Asuri yonis—
Not just of creatures, apes, beasts, brutes, monsters,
But amongst races, nations where Sanâtana-Dharma stays unheard,
He's cast midst darkened minds—that stay gripped in Nescience,
Where deceit is worn as perfume—and cannibals walk as humankind.

ॐ गीता श्लोकः १६.२० – GĪTĀ VERSE 16.20

ॐ श्रीमद्भगवद्गीतासूपनिषत्सु ब्रह्मविद्यायां योगशास्त्रे श्रीकृष्णार्जुनसंवादे
om śrīmadbhagavadgītāsūpaniṣatsu brahmavidyāyāṁ yogaśāstre śrīkṛṣṇārjunasaṁvāde
दैवासुरसम्पद्विभागयोगो नाम षोडशोऽध्यायः श्लोकः २०
daivāsurasampadvibhāgayogo nāma ṣoḍaśo'dhyāyaḥ ślokaḥ 20

— ॐ —

आसुरीं योनिमापन्ना मूढा जन्मनि जन्मनि ।
āsurīṁ yonimāpannā mūḍhā janmani janmani
मामप्राप्यैव कौन्तेय ततो यान्त्यधमां गतिम् ॥ १६-२० ॥
māmaprāpyaiva kaunteya tato yāntyadhamāṁ gatim (16-20)

Births after births, obtaining demoniac bodies and lives of delusional darkness, they keep sinking down into lower and still lower planes of existence—far from attaining Me. (16.20)

—: Word-by-Word :—

आसुरीम् āsurīm – demoniac; **योनिम्** yonim – wombs; **आपन्नाः** āpannāḥ – attaining; **मूढाः** mūḍhāḥ – the deluded ones; **जन्मनि जन्मनि** janmani janmani – birth after birth; **माम्** mām – Me; **अप्राप्य** eva aprāpya eva – failing to reach; **कौन्तेय** kaunteya – O son of Kunti; **ततः** tataḥ – thereafter; **यान्ति** yānti – they go; **अधमाम्** adhamām – to the lowest; **गतिम्** gatim – destination.

—: Understanding The Verse :—

— ॐ श्रीकृष्णाय नमः ॐ —

This profound and solemn verse forms the culmination of a somber sequence—wherein the Lord delineates the descent of those immersed in आसुरी-सम्पद् āsurī-sampad, the demoniac endowment.

Having portrayed the inner landscape of such beings—their arrogance, cruelty, and deluded grasping for transient pleasures—Shri Krishna now unveils the inexorable consequence of their course.

This verse speaks not merely of external downfall but of a progressive spiritual degradation, where each birth, squandered in ignorance and vice, draws the soul ever deeper into the abyss of saṁsāra, as if caught in a swirling vortex.

— ॐ श्रीरामाय नमः ॐ —

Ah! It's a tragic fate indeed—of those steeped in demoniac endowments.

- Doors to higher realms stay closed to them birth after birth.

- Among low-lifes they stay wandering—never reaching the light, never knowing peace.
- Each turn of the lock seals them deeper into the night.

The state of these souls, entrenched in the āsurī nature, appears most pitiable indeed, and their fall seemingly irreversible;
the Lord, ever the embodiment of boundless compassion, reveals this plight of theirs not as a pronouncement of doom—but as a merciful admonition to the rest—so that we ourselves never go down that path.

— ॐ ताटकान्तकाय नमः ॐ —

Here the human birth, a rare and precious attainment, stands as the appointed arena for self-transcendence and God-realization. Yet, when squandered under the sway of demoniac impulses, it becomes the very instrument of the soul's further entanglements.

These beings, unable to perceive the higher light, are drawn as if by an inner gravity into ever darker states—propelled not by the Lord's wrath but by the natural law of karma, the law of cause and effect that is innately woven into the fabric of creation.

This verse thus stands as both a solemn warning and a compassionate revelation, for in lifting the veil on the plight of the fallen, the Lord stirs the attentive soul to vigilance—urging him to turn toward the divine path while this precious opportunity of the rare human birth is still upon us.

— ॐ जनार्दनाय नमः ॐ —

In our next life—who knows what creature we will be born as!

The anserine—who mostly stays romanticizing and fantasizing themselves as having been born as a princess or knight, as someone great in their past life—know not of the unnumbered creature bodies they have donned upon their soul over the ages.

O dreamer, if everyone was a prince and princess the last time around—then who were the commonish humans that make up the bulk of humanity? And whence came all these animals—each of whom has a consciousness, and each one of whom has a soul—exactly like thine.

O wake up already fool—and specially watch out for what and whom ye eat.

—: Key Sanskrit Terms :—

— ॐ तत सत ॐ —

Let us rest with this verse as though before a sealed gate. The Sanskrit here speaks of long days and nights wasted, of doors staying unopened over many lifetimes—born a creature; yet even in its sternness the verse keeps alive the possibility of making a turnaround in the journey -- by taking to the right path.

Now let the verse teach us how to listen—not with the mind that grasps, but with the heart that opens. Just listen to the sounds of the Gītā shastra, and the Sanskrit will do the rest.

— ॐ —

आसुरीं योनिम् आपन्नाः (āsurīṁ yonim āpannāḥ)

- आसुरीं योनिम् Āsurīṁ yonim – the demoniac birth or condition. Here, yoni signifies more than just physical birth; it implies a mode of existence, a state of being dominated by tamas and rajas—hatred, ego, delusion, and absence of spiritual awareness.

- आपन्नाः Āpannāḥ – "attained" or "fallen into." This verb suggests not an uplifting evolution, but a descent into entangling conditions suited to one's inner constitution (bhāva).

The आसुरी योनि āsurī yoni thus represents not a punishment, but a natural gravitation toward one's karmic vibrations: **You wanted it, now you got it.**

— ॐ —

मूढाः (mūḍhāḥ)

From the root मू muh, "to be deluded", the term mūḍha signifies one whose intellect is clouded, whose discrimination (viveka) is veiled by ignorance (avidyā).

These are not merely intellectually ignorant but spiritually inert, unable to discern the imperishable Self from the perishable body and desires.

They are trapped in the dream-world of māyā, accepting falsehood as truth.

— ॐ —

जन्मनि जन्मनि (janmani janmani): "Birth after birth."

A powerful expression indicating the cyclicality of ignorance, wherein the soul is born again and again into conditions that perpetuate darkness.

These are recurrent patterns of bondage, not random rebirths but sequenced by saṁskāra and karma.

— ॐ —

माम् अप्राप्य एव (mām aprāpya eva)

- माम् Mām – referring to Shri Krishna as the Supreme Self, not merely the avatāra, but as satt-chitt-ānanda braham —the supreme absolute, He who is the ultimate goal of all spiritual effort.
- अप्राप्य Aprāpya – "not attaining," "failing to reach."
- एव Eva – adds emphasis: "certainly not," "indeed not."

Despite the opportunity of human birth, availability of scriptures, and the presence of the Lord in every heart, the asuras never turn toward Him—the very Source, the Creator and Sustainer of all existence.

— ॐ —

यान्ति अधमां गतिम् (yānti adhamāṁ gatim)

- यान्ति Yānti – they go, they proceed.
- अधमां गतिम् Adhamām gatim – "the most degraded state," the lowest spiritual condition.

Here गति gati does not merely mean destination; it connotes destiny, trajectory, or path.

The अधमा-गति adhamā-gati is not just rebirth in a lower realm—it signifies a deeper spiritual fall, further alienation from the Self, and immersion in darker veils of illusion.

—: *In Brief* :—

— ॐ श्रीकृष्णाय नमः ॐ —

Indeed, though such beings are fated—by the burdensome weight of their own dark tendencies—to descend into lower and lower births and even hellish states, it must be remembered that the human soul, by its very constitution, is endowed with the innate capacity for God-realization.

And this potential is not to taken lightly.

O mortal, this blessed opportunity of a human birth is not to be forfeited, be thrown away.

Despite the attainment of a human body, when one willfully turns away from the dharmic path and embraces the dark forces of delusion, lust, desire, greed—then one forfeits the supreme birthright as a human and continues his slide towards even darker destinies in one's long eonian journey.

— ॐ श्रीभगवते नमः ॐ —

The Lord's declaration that such souls, having repeatedly entered demoniac wombs, are cast down into frightful realms of suffering, should serve not merely to terrify us but to awaken us as well.

But even midst such grim portrayals, the Gītā ever holds aloft the light of hope.

The implication is clear: the soul must shun the base tendencies of काम kāma (desire), क्रोध krodha (anger), and लोभ lobha (greed), and cultivate the divine qualities that alone secure liberation.

— ॐ हरकोदण्ड खँडनाय नमः ॐ —

This verse serves as a transition toward the Lord's compassionate counsel which comes in the following śloka—wherein He discloses the underlying cause of such ruinous births and, by implication, the path of deliverance.

The earnest seeker is prepared to receive the Lord's urgent exhortation to abandon the triple gate of hell and walk the path that leads toward the supreme good: the emancipation of the soul, to get out of this dreadful birth-death cycle of sorrows.

— ॐ तत सत ॐ —

Before we move on, let us bow in reverence to this sacred verse—a timeless beacon of wisdom guiding seekers for ages. Write it by hand, reflect on its meaning, and chant it aloud, for these sounds alone carry the authenticity of that era. The world may have changed but the living vibration of these Sanskrit sounds still remain as original as they were when Bhagwān Shri Krishna Himself walked the earth and imparted these teachings.

— ॐ —

आसुरीं योनिमापन्ना मूढा जन्मनि जन्मनि ।
āsurīṁ yonimāpannā mūḍhā janmani janmani
मामप्राप्यैव कौन्तेय ततो यान्त्यधमां गतिम् ॥ १६-२० ॥
māmaprāpyaiva kaunteya tato yāntyadhamāṁ gatim (16-20)

— ॐ —
आसुरीं योनिमापन्ना मूढा जन्मनि जन्मनि ।
āsurīṁ yonimāpannā mūḍhā janmani janmani
मामप्राप्यैव कौन्तेय ततो यान्त्यधमां गतिम् ॥ १६-२० ॥
māmaprāpyaiva kaunteya tato yāntyadhamāṁ gatim (16-20)

ॐ तत्सदिति श्रीमद्भगवद्गीतासूपनिषत्सु ब्रह्मविद्यायां योगशास्त्रे श्रीकृष्णार्जुनसंवादे
om tatsaditi śrīmadbhagavadgītāsūpaniṣatsu brahmavidyāyāṁ yogaśāstre śrīkṛṣṇārjunasaṁvāde
दैवासुरसम्पद्विभागयोगो नाम षोडशोऽध्यायः श्लोकः २०
daivāsurasampadvibhāgayogo nāma ṣoḍaśo'dhyāyaḥ ślokaḥ 20

Om-Tat-Sat—Om (Braham) is the sole Reality. In the Yogic Scripture on the Science-of-Braham, the Shrimada-Bhāgvada-Gītā Upanishad, we hereby conclude Shloka 20 of the Dialogue between Shrī Krishna and Arjuna entitled Daivāsura-Sampada-Vibhāga-Yoga, Canto XVI.

ॐ गीता श्लोकः १६.२१ – GĪTĀ VERSE 16.21

ॐ श्रीमद्भगवद्गीतासूपनिषत्सु ब्रह्मविद्यायां योगशास्त्रे श्रीकृष्णार्जुनसंवादे
om śrīmadbhagavadgītāsūpaniṣatsu brahmavidyāyāṁ yogaśāstre śrīkṛṣṇārjunasaṁvāde
दैवासुरसम्पद्विभागयोगो नाम षोडशोऽध्यायः श्लोकः २१
daivāsurasampadvibhāgayogo nāma ṣoḍaśo'dhyāyaḥ ślokaḥ 21

— ॐ —

त्रिविधं नरकस्येदं द्वारं नाशनमात्मनः ।
trividhaṁ narakasyedaṁ dvāraṁ nāśanamātmanaḥ
कामः क्रोधस्तथा लोभस्तस्मादेतत्त्रयं त्यजेत् ॥१६-२१॥
kāmaḥ krodhastathā lobhastasmādetattrayaṁ tyajet (16-21)

Lust, anger, greed—the triple gateways to hell—are destructive of the self; therefore, one should carefully shun these three. (16.21)

—: Word-by-Word :—

त्रिविधम् trividham – threefold; **नरकस्य** narakasya – of hell; **इदम्** idam – this; **द्वारम्** dvāram – gate; **नाशनम्** nāśanam – destructive; **आत्मनः** ātmanaḥ – to the self; **कामः** kāmaḥ – desire; **क्रोधः** krodhaḥ – anger; **तथा** tathā – and; **लोभः** lobhaḥ – greed; **तस्मात्** tasmāt – therefore; **एतत्** etat – these; **त्रयम्** trayam – three; **त्यजेत्** tyajet – should be abandoned.

—: Understanding The Verse :—

— ॐ श्रीकृष्णाय नमः ॐ —

This śloka stands as a luminous pivot in the unfolding of Canto Sixteen. Having unveiled the ruinous fate of those steeped in āsurī-sampad, the demoniac endowment, Shri Krishna now distills into a single, powerful utterance the core afflictions that underlie such degeneration.

Here, the Lord identifies **काम-क्रोध -लोभ** kāma (lust), krodha (anger), and lobha (greed) as **the triple gateways** to Naraka, the hellish states of existence, not merely as external realms but as inward conditions that shroud the soul in darkness.

— ॐ श्रीरामाय नमः ॐ —

Lust, as the restless craving for fleeting pleasures;
Anger, as the fiery storm that erupts when desires are thwarted;
and **Greed**, the insatiable hunger for possession and accumulation —these **three are the root** from which the poisonous tree of spiritual downfall grows.

They corrupt thought, pollute speech, and degrade action, ensnaring the jīva deeper into the coils of saṁsāra.

Yet in this grim revelation lies also the implicit grace of the Lord, for in pointing to the cause, He silently opens the door to liberation.

To recognize and renounce these forces is to sever the bonds that tether the soul to its lower nature and to rise toward the divine heights of one's true being.

—: Key Sanskrit Terms :—

— ॐ तत सत ॐ —

The verse burns with three distinct flames: lust, anger, greed—which stand like glimmering flashlights at the threshold of the dark world, beckoning us to come in.

The Gītā verse names them plainly, and in thus naming gives us a warning, so that wise may walk away before entering.

The Sanskrit words appear here like lanterns in fog—distant at first, then glowing, then clear—each one illuminating a corner of meaning we hadn't noticed before.

— ॐ —

त्रिविधं (trividhaṁ): This means "threefold" or "of three kinds."

The term त्रिविधं tri-vidhaṁ denotes a triple formation of destructive forces that, though distinct, often arise interdependently—forming a triad of binding passions.

This darkly trinity is well-attested in the sanātani śāstras as inimical to spiritual life.

— ॐ —

नरकस्य इदं द्वारं (narakasya idaṁ dvāraṁ)

- नरक Naraka – often translated as "hell," yet it fundamentally means a state of existential suffering, where ignorance (avidyā), separation from the Self, and bondage to tamas prevail.

- द्वार Dvāraṁ – "doorway" or "gateway."

These three—काम क्रोध लोभ kāma, krodha, lobha—are not नरक Naraka in itself but are portals through which one enters the realm of inner ruin and spiritual darkness.

Shri Krishna is thus stating not only a moral truth but a cosmic psychology—these qualities are entry points into degradation of the Self.

— ॐ —

नाशनम् आत्मनः (nāśanam ātmanaḥ)

- नाशनम् Nāśanam – destruction, dissolution, loss.
- आत्मनः Ātmanaḥ – of the self.

Here, आत्मनः "ātmanaḥ" refers not to the eternal आत्मा Ātmā —which is indestructible—but to the lower self, the jīva's identification with body, mind, and ego.

Thus, नाशनम् आत्मनः nāśanam ātmanaḥ means the annihilation of the soul's clarity, of its dharmic integrity, and of its upward spiritual momentum.

These three forces fully consume the merit (puṇya), wisdom (jñāna), and peace (śānti) of the individual.

— ॐ —

कामः, क्रोधः, लोभः (kāmaḥ, krodhaḥ, lobhaḥ)

These toxicities, the three poisons, are also echoed in the Upaniṣads and later in the Buddhist and Jain traditions:

- कामः Kāmaḥ – Desire, not merely physical lust, but compulsive craving—the root of attachment (saṅga) and the seed of suffering.
- क्रोधः Krodhaḥ – Anger, which arises when kāma is obstructed. It clouds discernment and breeds violence of speech, thought, and action.
- लोभः Lobhaḥ – Greed, an insatiable grasping for more, arising from delusion that external accumulation can fulfill the Self.

Each of these chains the soul to saṁsāra, and together they form a formidable wall against Self-realization.

— ॐ —

तस्मात् एतत् त्रयं त्यजेत् (tasmād etat trayaṁ tyajet)

- तस्मात् Tasmāt – therefore, hence.
- एतत् Etat trayaṁ – this triad.
- त्यजेत् Tyajet – one should abandon, renounce, discard.

The verb त्यजेत् tyajet is in the injunctive mood—a command imbued with both urgency and sacred counsel.

This is not mere casual advice but the very prescription for liberation: the deliberate and conscious rejection of these three tendencies is essential to escape the downward pull of नरक Naraka.

— ॐ —

Thus this verse warns us about the three burning flames which consume the world: lust, anger, greed—hell's triple gates yawning wide—with each spark of the verse a dire Warning that blazes at the threshold to caution us before we foolishly enter into veritable Hell.

—: In Brief :—

— ॐ श्रीकृष्णाय नमः ॐ —

Desire, anger, and greed—this triad of ruin—is the gateway through which the soul enters into its own undoing.

As the verse reveals, these forces precipitate not only external misfortune but the inner corrosion of the soul's divine potential.

काम Kāma drives one to sinful indulgence;
क्रोध krodha consumes one in the fires of violence and resentment;
and लोभ obha binds one in the endless pursuit of wealth, blinding the intellect and defiling the heart.

Their cumulative effect is the progressive obscuration of the soul's innate purity, its fall from dharma, and its descent into realms of sufferings, not just here but also hereafter—in the afterlife.

— ॐ दण्डकारण्य पुण्यकृते नमः ॐ —

It is for this reason that Bhagwāna Shri Krishna, in His compassionate wisdom, exhorts us to shun these three as one would avoid a deadly toxin.

The term आत्मनः "ātmanah" here signifies the embodied self, whose true nature is not annihilated but obscured, corrupted, and veiled by these passions.

By forsaking काम क्रोध लोभ kāma, krodha, and lobha, one safeguards the sanctity of life, preserves the light of reason, and nurtures the seeds of spiritual awakening. The path of renunciation is not only that of sterile negation, but of luminous liberation.

In the next verse, the Lord will turn from this solemn warning to an uplifting declaration, extolling the glory of the one who, freed from these triple gates of hell, walks the noble path of self-mastery and attains the supreme goal.

The teaching will now move from peril to promise—from warning to benediction.

— ॐ तत सत ॐ —

Before we move on, let us bow in reverence to this sacred verse—a timeless beacon of wisdom guiding seekers for ages. Write it by hand, reflect on its meaning, and chant it aloud, for these sounds alone carry the authenticity of that era. The world may have changed but the living vibration of these Sanskrit sounds still remain as original as they were when Bhagwān Shri Krishna Himself walked the earth and imparted these teachings.

— ॐ —

त्रिविधं नरकस्येदं द्वारं नाशनमात्मनः ।
trividhaṁ narakasyedaṁ dvāraṁ nāśanamātmanaḥ
कामः क्रोधस्तथा लोभस्तस्मादेतत्त्रयं त्यजेत् ॥ १६-२१ ॥
kāmaḥ krodhastathā lobhastasmādetattrayaṁ tyajet (16-21)

त्रिविधं नरकस्येदं द्वारं नाशनमात्मनः ।
trividhaṁ narakasyedaṁ dvāraṁ nāśanamātmanaḥ
कामः क्रोधस्तथा लोभस्तस्मादेतत्त्रयं त्यजेत् ॥ १६-२१ ॥
kāmaḥ krodhastathā lobhastasmādetattrayaṁ tyajet (16-21)

ॐ तत्सदिति श्रीमद्भगवद्गीतासूपनिषत्सु ब्रह्मविद्यायां योगशास्त्रे श्रीकृष्णार्जुनसंवादे
om tatsaditi śrīmadbhagavadgītāsūpaniṣatsu brahmavidyāyāṁ yogaśāstre śrīkṛṣṇārjunasaṁvāde
दैवासुरसम्पद्विभागयोगो नाम षोडशोऽध्यायः श्लोकः २१
daivāsurasampadvibhāgayogo nāma ṣoḍaśo'dhyāyaḥ ślokaḥ 21

Om-Tat-Sat—Om (Braham) is the sole Reality. In the Yogic Scripture on the Science-of-Braham, the Shrimada-Bhāgvada-Gītā Upanishad, we hereby conclude Shloka 21 of the Dialogue between Shrī Krishna and Arjuna entitled Daivāsura-Sampada-Vibhāga-Yoga, Canto XVI.

<u>त्रिविधं नरकस्य द्वारं The Triple Gateway to *Naraka*—Hell</u>

O me, O trembling soul, how oft I crossed those gates,
Where kâma sang, and krodha burned, and lobha sealed my fate.
काम क्रोध लोभ Three demons clothed in finery stood smiling at my side,
They promised joy—but led me down to lands where light stayed died.

Desire unchained became my law—I worshiped what decays,
And when denied—my wrath flared high, torching the bridge to wiser ways.
Then greed arrived, its hunger vast—devouring all I knew,
And I—so blind—fed it even more, till all I touched turned blue.

O soul, dost thou not see? These three are poisons sweet—
Each sip a vow to नरक Naraka—each step a chain on thy feet.

<u>But the Lord, who Closes the Named Gates, also Opens other Doors.</u>

Lo! The Lord in love reveals the gateways I must flee,
Not wrathful His teaching—He seeks to set me free.
He names the threefold bondage—not to bind, but to unbind,
He marks the path of ruin—so may choose the right: Sanâtani kind.

O soul, Krishna does not curse thee—He holds a mirror high,
That seeing thine old wounds—thou mayest learn to repent/cry.
To know of Enemy is be Graced. To tell of Thief is to bring us Light,
Now that I see the triple gates—I must turn from falling into blight.
So thank the Lord who strikes with Truth—not with Sword or Rod,
For He hath shown the poison's name—and called thee back to God.

ॐ गीता श्लोकः १६.२२ – Gītā Verse 16.22

ॐ श्रीमद्भगवद्गीतासूपनिषत्सु ब्रह्मविद्यायां योगशास्त्रे श्रीकृष्णार्जुनसंवादे
om śrīmadbhagavadgītāsūpaniṣatsu brahmavidyāyāṁ yogaśāstre śrīkṛṣṇārjunasaṁvāde
दैवासुरसम्पद्विभागयोगो नाम षोडशोऽध्यायः श्लोकः २२
daivāsurasampadvibhāgayogo nāma ṣoḍaśo'dhyāyaḥ ślokaḥ 22

— ॐ —

एतैर्विमुक्तः कौन्तेय तमोद्वारैस्त्रिभिर्नरः ।
etairvimuktaḥ kaunteya tamodvāraistribhirnaraḥ
आचरत्यात्मनः श्रेयस्ततो याति परां गतिम् ॥ १६-२२ ॥
ācaratyātmanaḥ śreyastato yāti parāṁ gatim (16-22)

Whosoever manages to thwart these three gates of hell, is able to pursue what is good for the self—working for his own salvation and eventually reaching the supreme state. (16.22)

—: Word-by-Word :—

एतैः etaiḥ – from these; **विमुक्तः** vimuktaḥ – freed; **कौन्तेय** kaunteya – O son of Kunti; **तमोद्वारैः** tamo-dvāraiḥ – the gates of darkness; **त्रिभिः** tribhiḥ – the three; **नरः** naraḥ – a person; **आचरति** ācarati – acts; **आत्मनः** ātmanaḥ – for the self's; **श्रेयः** śreyas – ultimate good; **ततः** tataḥ – thereby; **याति** yāti – attains; **पराम्** parām – the supreme; **गतिम्** gatim – destination.

—: Understanding The Verse :—

— ॐ श्रीकृष्णाय नमः ॐ —

This verse marks the Lord's gracious transition from the somber portrait of spiritual downfall to the luminous promise of deliverance.

Having declared the destructive power of kāma, krodha, and lobha—lust, anger, and greed—as the triple portals to hellish states, Shri Krishna now reveals the transformative potential latent in the human soul: the capacity for conscious renunciation.

Importantly take note: the Lord does not merely advocate rejection, but points toward elevation.

— ॐ श्रीरामाय नमः ॐ —

Renunciation here is not barren withdrawal, rather it is the liberation of the soul from the fetters that obscure his divine nature.

The one who rises above these dark impulses sets foot upon the path of śreyas—the highest good—striving for self-upliftment and ultimately ascending to the supreme state: mokṣa – which is the ultimate realization: of who-I-am.

— ॐ श्रीनारायणाय नमः ॐ —

Who am I? I am He.

"That One I am"—to know that is self-realization.

That is moksha. That is Nirvana: realizing I am not merely the wave but the ocean, that I am one within satt-chitt-ānanda braham—the ocean of existence-bliss-consciousness.

— ॐ सुग्रीवेप्सित राज्यदाय नमः ॐ —

This verse also underscores a profound teaching: that a man's dignity as नर nara—as a decent human being—is not defined merely by form, but by the nobility of striving for spiritual emancipation—and ultimately realizing, in one blessed birth: that I too am He, verily नारायण nārāyaṇa.

But that is the very pinnacle of the soul's journey, needing many, many births, not within easy reach, and we are so far away from that exalted state; meanwhile, the first thing is to conquer these gateways of darkness—to awaken the soul's innate luminosity and prepare it for union with the Divine.

—: Key Sanskrit Terms :—

— ॐ तत सत ॐ —

We see how the verse has softened here. Its words flows like rain falling on scorched earth—each sound carrying coolness, renewal, release.

Come let us linger here—for the Sanskrit words are waters that cleanse and restore. Let's not try to grasp at them—let it just happen.

Let the Sanskrit unfold itself like an old song remembered in pieces—part rhythm, part echo, part ache.

— ॐ —

एतैः विमुक्तः (etair vimuktaḥ)

- **एतैः** Etaiḥ – "from these," referring directly to the previously mentioned triad: **काम क्रोध लोभ** kāma (desire), krodha (anger), and lobha (greed).

- **विमुक्तः** Vimuktaḥ – "freed," "liberated."

This is not accidental release—it implies deliberate transcendence, the soul having actively disengaged from these binding forces.

The prefix '**वि** vi'- in '**विमुक्** vimukta' adds intensity: a complete, conscious liberation.

— ॐ —

कौन्तेय (kaunteya) An affectionate address—"O son of Kuntī"

This is Krishna' way to remind Arjuna (and the Arjuna in us) of his noble lineage and inner capacity for heroism.

This not merely a call to philosophical insight but to moral and spiritual courage.

— ॐ —

तमोद्वारैः त्रिभिः (tamodvāraiḥ tribhiḥ)

- तम Tamas – the guṇa of darkness, inertia, ignorance.
- द्वार Dvāra – gateway or entrance.
- त्रिभिः Tribhiḥ – the three: kāma, krodha, lobha.

These three (काम क्रोध लोभ kāma krodha lobha) are not just negative tendencies; they are entry-points into tamas, into the state where the soul forgets its luminous origin and dwells in the shadows of ego, sense-clinging, and delusion.

To be freed from them is to rise above rajas and tamas—into the realm of sattva.

— ॐ —

नरः आचरति आत्मनः श्रेयः (naraḥ ācarati ātmanaḥ śreyas)

- नरः Naraḥ – man, human being, the conscious seeker.
- आचरति Ācarati – acts, lives, conducts oneself.
- आत्मनः Ātmanaḥ – for the Self, meaning both the empirical self (jīva) and the essential Self (Ātmā).
- श्रेयः Śreyas – the higher good, the auspicious, the supreme welfare.

श्रेय Śreyas is a loaded term in Vedānta. It contrasts with प्रिय preyas—that which is sensory—pleasant, but transient.

Here, आचरति आत्मनः श्रेयः ācarati ātmanaḥ śreyas means: one lives a life aligned with the true, eternal welfare of the soul.

— ॐ —

ततः याति परां गतिम् (tataḥ yāti parāṁ gatim)

- ततः Tataḥ – from that, as a consequence.
- याति Yāti – goes, attains, reaches.
- परां गतिम् Parām gatim – the supreme goal or final destination.

परा गति Parā gati refers to liberation मोक्ष (mokṣa)—the highest spiritual state wherein the soul abides in its unconditioned nature, free from संसार saṁsāra, beyond rebirth, and innately established in satt-chitt-ānanda braham.

—: In Brief :—

Even acts that outwardly appear virtuous—be it sacrifice, charity, or worship—if impelled by selfish craving, pride, avarice, ire, desire become tainted and fail to yield true spiritual fruit.

Therefore, each sincere aspirant must vigilantly renounce these inner enemies, recognizing them as the seeds of sin and of one's ruin, and the ruin of Sanātana-Dharma. Aye, it's not only inward erosion of purity, peace, and God-consciousness which is caused by these, but also the outward rupture of social harmony and disruptions within society.

— ॐ श्रीरामाय नमः ॐ —

To be free from desire, anger, and greed is not merely to suppress them, but to uproot their sway from within—remove the burning ember from one's very heart.

Cool rain sometimes follows fire, and he who turns from these 'portal-to-hell', has started to walk the path of freedom in Gītā-Dharma—with each word, each verse of the Gītā-shastra like a raindrop of nectar -- soothing, restoring, redeeming.

— ॐ पीतवाससे नमः ॐ —

Those of divine disposition—even though surrounded by the misunderstandings and scorns of the worldly-minded—remain ever steadfast in their quest for the highest good.

Their hearts brim with compassion, and they do not harbor malice toward those ensnared in the demoniac nature; rather, they pray for their awakening—unless they become a menace to the world and must needs be uprooted.

To keep the garden a garden, the weed must be regularly weeded out—or the whole thing becomes an inhabitable wilderness.

And it is for this reason that Krishna points to the adharmic forces standing before and tells Arjuna: Eradicate.

Nay, not out of anger, nor out of desire for riches, nor to ravage them driven by lust for their wealth or women—but only for the sake of restoring the cosmic order, for the greater good of righteousness, for the safekeeping of Sanātana-Dharma, for the welfare of the simple good folks of the world.

In a way the verse celebrates the greatness of those who, through inner renunciation, work for their own salvation—and by extension, contribute to the welfare of the world.

— ॐ श्रीमते नमः ॐ —

As we stand at this juncture in the teaching, a natural question arises: what of those who, disregarding scriptural guidance, act according to their own whims and subjective notions of right and wrong? Do they too reach the supreme goal, or do they remain bound?

Anticipating this inquiry, the Lord, in the next verse, illumines the destiny of such self-willed actors, offering further clarity on the role of śāstra and divine ordinance in the soul's journey toward perfection.

— ॐ तत सत ॐ —

Before moving on, let us once more bow in deep reverence before this sacred verse of the Bhagavad-Gītā, an eternal beacon of wisdom that ceaselessly illumines the path of seekers. Engage with its form—inscribe it with your own hand, let your heart dwell upon its meaning, and raise your voice in its chanting—for within these syllables echoes the undying proclamation delivered millennia ago on the battlefield of Kurukshetra. These words, transmitted unchanged across the unbroken chain of generations, form a living bridge, linking us to that sanctified era when Bhagwāna Shri Krishna Himself walked this earth and bestowed this divine teaching. Through the luminous vibration of these sacred Sanskrit sounds, we are drawn nearer to His timeless presence, touching the very heartbeat of the Eternal.

— ॐ —

एतैर्विमुक्तः कौन्तेय तमोद्वारैस्त्रिभिर्नरः ।
etairvimuktaḥ kaunteya tamodvāraistribhirnaraḥ
आचरत्यात्मनः श्रेयस्ततो याति परां गतिम् ॥ १६-२२ ॥
ācaratyātmanaḥ śreyastato yāti parāṁ gatim (16-22)

— ॐ —

एतैर्विमुक्तः कौन्तेय तमोद्वारैस्त्रिभिर्नरः ।
etairvimuktaḥ kaunteya tamodvāraistribhirnaraḥ
आचरत्यात्मनः श्रेयस्ततो याति परां गतिम् ॥ १६-२२ ॥
ācaratyātmanaḥ śreyastato yāti parāṁ gatim (16-22)

ॐ तत्सदिति श्रीमद्भगवद्गीतासूपनिषत्सु ब्रह्मविद्यायां योगशास्त्रे श्रीकृष्णार्जुनसंवादे
om tatsaditi śrīmadbhagavadgītāsūpaniṣatsu brahmavidyāyāṁ yogaśāstre śrīkṛṣṇārjunasaṁvāde
दैवासुरसम्पद्विभागयोगो नाम षोडशोऽध्यायः श्लोकः २२
daivāsurasampadvibhāgayogo nāma ṣoḍaśo'dhyāyaḥ ślokaḥ 22

Om-Tat-Sat—Om (Braham) is the sole Reality. In the Yogic Scripture on the Science-of-Braham, the Shrimada-Bhāgvada-Gītā Upanishad, we hereby conclude Shloka 22 of the Dialogue between Shrī Krishna and Arjuna entitled Daivāsura-Sampada-Vibhāga-Yoga, Canto XVI.

ॐ गीता श्लोकः १६.२३ – GĪTĀ VERSE 16.23

ॐ श्रीमद्भगवद्गीतासूपनिषत्सु ब्रह्मविद्यायां योगशास्त्रे श्रीकृष्णार्जुनसंवादे
om śrīmadbhagavadgītāsūpaniṣatsu brahmavidyāyāṁ yogaśāstre śrīkṛṣṇārjunasaṁvāde
दैवासुरसम्पद्विभागयोगो नाम षोडशोऽध्यायः श्लोकः २३
daivāsurasampadvibhāgayogo nāma ṣoḍaśo'dhyāyaḥ ślokaḥ 23

— ॐ —

यः शास्त्रविधिमुत्सृज्य वर्तते कामकारतः ।
yaḥ śāstravidhimutsṛjya vartate kāmakārataḥ
न स सिद्धिमवाप्नोति न सुखं न परां गतिम् ॥ १६-२३ ॥
na sa siddhimavāpnoti na sukhaṁ na parāṁ gatim (16-23)

But setting aside the injunctions of the scriptures, he who instead acts simply under the impulses of desires—attains neither perfection, nor happiness, nor the supreme goal. (16.23)

—: *Word-by-Word* :—

यः yaḥ – who; **शास्त्रविधिम्** śāstra-vidhim – the injunctions of the scriptures; **उत्सृज्य** utsṛjya – disregarding; **वर्तते** vartate – acts; **कामकारतः** kāma-kārataḥ – according to their desires; **न** na – neither; **सः** saḥ – he; **सिद्धिम्** siddhim – perfection; **अवाप्नोति** avāpnoti – attains; **न** na – nor; **सुखम्** sukham – happiness; **न** na – nor; **पराम्** parām – the supreme; **गतिम्** gatim – destination.

—: *Understanding The Verse* :—

— ॐ श्रीकृष्णाय नमः ॐ —

This verse stands as a solemn seal upon the teachings of Canto-Sixteen, offering a piercing insight into one of the most fundamental pillars of Sanātana-Dharma: **the supremacy of śāstras**, the sacred texts, as the beacon of human conduct and spiritual evolution.

Shri Krishna here draws a sharp and uncompromising distinction between the path illuminated by scriptural wisdom and the path clouded by self-will and unchecked desire.

— ॐ सुन्दराय नमः ॐ —

While the preceding verses delineated the demoniac tendencies and their ruinous consequences, this verse points to the root from which such tendencies spring: the rejection of divine guidance, the willful abandonment of the śāstric light in favor of the ego's impulses.

Actions undertaken in such a spirit, no matter how outwardly impressive or seemingly virtuous, are hollow at their core.

They do not lead to सिद्धि siddhi (perfection), सुख sukha (happiness), or परम गति paraṁ gati (the supreme goal)—because they lack the foundation of Sanātana-Dharma.

Pride transforms virtue into vice;
craving taints renunciation;
and the pursuit of pleasure binds rather than frees.

This verse thus emphasizes that it is not the outer form of action but the inner alignment with eternal principles that determines the soul's true progress.

— ॐ जितवाराशये नमः ॐ —

This śloka opens as to a path which has, alas, become abandoned to weeds through neglect and lethargy. The words whispers of those who forsake sacred counsel, and in that forsaking lose their way. Yet even here, in exile, the voice of Krishna calls us gently back.

Those of us who have perchance strayed, let us find our way back home—because the fool who rejects sacred counsel ends up getting completely ruined.

Such ones, continue to wander without rest in this world of sorrows. Ruled by self-will, lust, desire, these people find no perfection, no peace—their life an exile upon a thorny deserted path.

—: Key Sanskrit Terms :—

Come now, let us behold the verse as a woven tapestry and trace its hidden design by way of the luminous Sanskrit strands that hold its truths of Gītā-Dharma firmly in place.

— ॐ —

यः शास्त्रविधिम् उत्सृज्य (yaḥ śāstra-vidhim utsṛjya)
- यः Yaḥ – "he who" (referring to any person who…).
- शास्त्र-विधिम् Śāstra-vidhim – "the injunctions of the śāstra."
- शास्त्र Śāstra refers to sacred scripture: the Vedas and Vedanta; Smṛtis like the Manu-Smṛti; Itihasas like the Mahabharata and Ramayana; the Purāṇas—texts that articulate the principles of Sanātana-Dharma.

And of course the Bhagavad-Gītā itself is now the most-important शास्त्र Śāstra after Bhagwāna Shri Krishna revealed it.

- विधि Vidhi denotes prescribed rule or sacred injunction.
- उत्सृज्य Utsṛjya – "abandoning," "discarding," "casting aside."

Thus, this phrase marks a person who, out of pride, delusion, or disregard, chooses to act in rejection of divine ordinance—which in the traditional world-view is not just rule-breaking but a violation of cosmic harmony (ऋत ṛta).

— ॐ —

वर्तते कामकारतः (vartate kāmakārataḥ)
- वर्तते Vartate – “he lives,” “conducts himself,” “acts.”
- कामकारतः Kāmakārataḥ – “according to the impulse of desire” (from काम kāma - desire, and कारतः kārataḥ - driven by, in the manner of).

This implies a life governed not by reason, revelation, or renunciation, but by the whim of ungoverned longing. Such a person is impelled, not guided, by the senses and passions.

— ॐ —

न स सिद्धिम् अवाप्नोति (na sa siddhim avāpnoti)
- न स Na sa – “he does not”
- सिद्धिम् Siddhim – “perfection” or “accomplishment.”

In the Gītā, this implies:

- Spiritual attainment,
- Purity of mind,
- Mastery over the lower self,
- Realization of the Self.

Such a person, acting against शास्त्र śāstra, fails to attain any lasting fulfillment—in this life or beyond.

— ॐ —

न सुखं (na sukham)
- सुखं Sukham – joy, peace, contentment.

He neither attains outer joy nor inner peace.

सुख Sukha, derived from सु su- ख kha (good-space), implies an unobstructed inner condition, an inner harmony in tune with the divine.

When one violates the natural law of dharma, that harmony gets broken.

— ॐ —

न परां गतिम् (na parāṁ gatim)
- परा गति Parā gati – the supreme goal: मोक्ष Mokṣa, the highest destiny, liberation from संसार saṁsāra.

Acting against शास्त्र śāstra does शास्त्र not only deny worldly success—it cuts the seeker off from spiritual ascent, from the very purpose of human birth.

—: In Brief :—

— ॐ श्रीकृष्णाय नमः ॐ —

He who disregards the injunctions of the शास्त्र śāstras and acts according to his own whims—driven by self-will, ambition, or pride—finds neither perfection nor peace, neither fulfillment in this world nor the attainment of the Supreme.

The term शास्त्र śāstra encompasses the Vedas, the Smṛtis, the Purāṇas, the Itihāsas—the entire body of sacred lore that constitutes the revealed wisdom of the ages, pointing the soul toward the good, the true, and the eternal.

It is from these texts that one learns of Sanātana-Dharma, and of the art of renouncing the demoniac dispositions and cultivating the divine virtues that lead to liberation.

Of all the śāstras, the Bhagavad-Gītā today is the most important. The Bhagavad-Gītā encapsulates the entirety of Sanātana-Dharma—it is the sutra-grantha.

And when you take the shelter of Bhagavad-Gītā—you have it all and you need nothing else.

— ॐ हृषीकेशाय नमः ॐ —

To flout this guidance and follow the dictates of mere personal reasoning, colored by desire or the craving for honor and fame, is to sever oneself from the current of grace that flows through Sanātana-Dharma.

Such arbitrary acts, even when not expressly sinful, become barren, for they lack the sanction of higher wisdom.

Thus, far from attaining the supreme goal, the self-willed actor gains not even the lesser rewards—whether worldly happiness or occult perfections. His path becomes a wandering in the wilderness of restlessness, bearing no lasting fruit.

— ॐ वैदेहीप्रियाय नमः ॐ —

This declaration may naturally stir a question in the reflective heart: if arbitrary action leads only to ruin, then by what principle should a man guide his life?

Anticipating this profound query, the Lord, in the next verse, turns to reveal the true standard by which human action must be measured, pointing once again to the शास्त्र śāstras of Ekam-Sanātana-Dharma as the guiding light and refuge for the sincere aspirant.

— ॐ तत सत ॐ —

Before we move on, let us bow in reverence to this sacred verse. Write it by hand, reflect on its meaning, chant it aloud, make it your own.

— ॐ —

यः शास्त्रविधिमुत्सृज्य वर्तते कामकारतः ।
yaḥ śāstravidhimutsṛjya vartate kāmakārataḥ
न स सिद्धिमवाप्नोति न सुखं न परां गतिम् ॥१६-२३॥
na sa siddhimavāpnoti na sukhaṁ na parāṁ gatim (16-23)

— ॐ —

यः शास्त्रविधिमुत्सृज्य वर्तते कामकारतः ।
yaḥ śāstravidhimutsṛjya vartate kāmakārataḥ
न स सिद्धिमवाप्नोति न सुखं न परां गतिम् ॥१६-२३॥
na sa siddhimavāpnoti na sukhaṁ na parāṁ gatim (16-23)

ॐ तत्सदिति श्रीमद्भगवद्गीतासूपनिषत्सु ब्रह्मविद्यायां योगशास्त्रे श्रीकृष्णार्जुनसंवादे
om tatsaditi śrīmadbhagavadgītāsūpaniṣatsu brahmavidyāyāṁ yogaśāstre śrīkṛṣṇārjunasaṁvāde
दैवासुरसम्पद्विभागयोगो नाम षोडशोऽध्यायः श्लोकः २३
daivāsurasampadvibhāgayogo nāma ṣoḍaśo'dhyāyaḥ ślokaḥ 23

Om-Tat-Sat—Om (Braham) is the sole Reality. In the Yogic Scripture on the Science-of-Braham, the Shrimada-Bhāgvada-Gītā Upanishad, we hereby conclude Shloka 23 of the Dialogue between Shrī Krishna and Arjuna entitled Daivāsura-Sampada-Vibhāga-Yoga, Canto XVI.

शास्त्र Śāstra: the Mirror That Warns and Guides

O Krishna, Thou showed us the darker side
—not as One who delights in shadows—
But to name them, illumine them for us—for us to pass beyond !

O Mortal, Do not despair to hear these āsuri traits,
nor run away from what, in the mirror, we may have seen—
For the Gita sings not to condemn—but to call us seekers Home.

The āsuric is not eternally doomed—but selfsame Ātmā in sleep's disguise;
Every night—when known to be such—prepares a inward morning rise.

Each vice is but a veil still unpierced—a divine-flame, not rightly fed,
And he who sees his fault rightly, eventually gets to lift his fallen head.

Sanātana-Dharma speaks in hope, in love—
It instructs in Laws that are designed to heal—
And through discernment's quiet Might, one can again turn the Wheel.

The turnaround starts by knowing of these darkly shadows—
and then begin walking in Dharma, following the all important Shastra:
the Bhagavad-Gītā Śāstra शास्त्र of Lord-God Bhagwāna Krishna Himself.

ॐ गीता श्लोकः १६.२४ – GĪTĀ VERSE 16.24

ॐ श्रीमद्भगवद्गीतासूपनिषत्सु ब्रह्मविद्यायां योगशास्त्रे श्रीकृष्णार्जुनसंवादे
om śrīmadbhagavadgītāsūpaniṣatsu brahmavidyāyāṁ yogaśāstre śrīkṛṣṇārjunasaṁvāde
दैवासुरसम्पद्विभागयोगो नाम षोडशोऽध्यायः श्लोकः २४
daivāsurasampadvibhāgayogo nāma ṣoḍaśo'dhyāyaḥ ślokaḥ 24

— ॐ —

तस्माच्छास्त्रं प्रमाणं ते कार्याकार्यव्यवस्थितौ ।
tasmācchāstraṁ pramāṇaṁ te kāryākāryavyavasthitau
ज्ञात्वा शास्त्रविधानोक्तं कर्म कर्तुमिहार्हसि ॥१६-२४॥
jñātvā śāstravidhānoktaṁ karma kartumihārhasi (16-24)

So let the scriptures be your authority in ascertaining what ought to be done and what ought not to be done; and thus knowing that which is prescribed in the scriptures—act accordingly." (16.24)

—: Word-by-Word :—

तस्मात् tasmāt – therefore; **शास्त्रम्** śāstram – scripture; **प्रमाणम्** pramāṇam – the authority; **ते** te – for you; **कार्याकार्यव्यवस्थितौ** kārya-akārya-vyavasthitau – in determining what is to be done and what is not to be done; **ज्ञात्वा** jñātvā – knowing; **शास्त्रविधानोक्तम्** śāstra-vidhāna-uktam – as enjoined in the scriptures; **कर्म** karma – action; **कर्तुम्** kartum – to perform; **इह** iha – here; **अर्हसि** arhasi – you ought.

—: Understanding The Verse :—

— ॐ श्रीकृष्णाय नमः ॐ —

This closing verse of Chapter 16 serves as the culminating injunction of the entire Canto—a luminous affirmation of the indispensable role of śāstras, the scriptures of Sanātana-Dharma in man's spiritual journey.

When Shri Krishna was speaking this verse, the Gītā was still work in progress, but of course now the Bhagavad-Gitā stands as the foremost of all śāstras, the holiest of all holy scriptures—for it comes to us straight from the lips of Lord-God Bhagwāna Himself.

— ॐ श्रीरामाय नमः ॐ —

Having vividly described the downward pull of demoniac tendencies and the ruin wrought by heedless, self-willed actions, Shri Krishna turns in this verse to deliver a clarion command to the earnest seeker: let the **शास्त्र** śāstra be your **प्रमाण** pramāṇa—your highest standard, your authoritative measure in discerning right from wrong, the path to follow and the path to shun.

This verse underscores a vital principle of Sanātana-Dharma: Human understanding and wants, though valuable, are not self-sufficient when untethered from the timeless wisdom enshrined in the sacred scriptures.

— ॐ परमपुरुषाय नमः ॐ —

Left to the sway of desires and fleeting impulses, man loses his way; but illumined by scriptural light, following the path of Gītā-Dharma, he finds the sure path to Sanātana-Dharma, inner peace, and ultimate liberation.

The scriptures stand not as mere external codes, but as a divine compass, aligning the individual with cosmic order, awakening man to his true nature, and guiding him toward the Supreme Goal.

Thusly the Lord, out of His compassion, instructs Arjuna—and through him all of us —that the key to human flourishing lies in harmonizing one's life with the eternal truths revealed in the शास्त्र śāstras—the authentic scriptures of Sanātana-Dharma—meaning only those which are from Shri Krishna's time and before.

—: Key Sanskrit Terms :—

This beautiful verse of canto-sixteen graciously places a timeless lamp upon our path—its Sanskrit words like the steady flames that continue to guide us step by step. Let us begin with them as with light itself—sure, unwavering, and sufficient to carry us forward.

Now let us attend to the central Sanskrit expressions of the verse, allowing them to open like windows—framing vistas of thought, feeling, ancient wisdom and the intention of God.

— ॐ —

तस्मात् (tasmāt): "Therefore."

This term draws a direct conclusion from the preceding verse (16.23). Since acting apart from śāstra leads to no सिद्धि siddhi, सुख sukha, or परा-गति parā gati, therefore one must abide by scriptural guidance.

This is a very must. This is the logical and spiritual necessity born from the law of dharma.

— ॐ —

शास्त्रं प्रमाणं ते (śāstraṁ pramāṇaṁ te)

- शास्त्रं Śāstraṁ – Scripture; divine law, revealed truth.

- प्रमाणं Pramāṇaṁ – Measure, standard, authority; that which establishes valid knowledge (pramā).
- ते Te – for you (Arjuna, and by extension, all seekers).

This is the heart of the verse: शास्त्र śāstra is declared as the supreme प्रमाण pramāṇa in determining कार्य kārya (what should be done) and अकार्य akārya (what should not be done).

प्रमाण Pramāṇa in Sanātana philosophy is that which leads to right knowledge, and in the realm of action, this means action in harmony with the eternal dharma.

— ॐ —

कार्याकार्यव्यवस्थितौ (kāryākāryavyavasthitau)

- कार्य Kārya – That which is to be done; duty, righteous action.
- अकार्य Akārya – That which is not to be done; prohibited or unrighteous action.
- व्यवस्थितौ Vyavasthitau – In the determination or discernment.

The verse enjoins all seekers to turn to शास्त्र śāstra to discern the fine line between righteousness and error, between actions that liberate and those that blind and bind.

— ॐ —

ज्ञात्वा शास्त्रविधानोक्तं (jñātvā śāstra-vidhāna-uktam)

- ज्ञात्वा Jñātvā – Having known, understood.
- शास्त्रविधानोक्तं Śāstra-vidhāna-uktam – That which is spoken or prescribed by śāstra through its ordinance.
- It is not enough to merely revere शास्त्र śāstras—one must understand them.
- Knowledge (jñāna) precedes action (karma)—so make sure that that impelling knowledge is right and refined.

The Gītā advocates not blind conformity but illumined obedience, rooted in:

- study अध्ययन (adhyayana),
- reflection मनन (manana), and
- assimilation निदिध्यासन (nididhyāsana) of śāstric teaching.

— ॐ —

कर्म कर्तुम् इह अर्हसि (karma kartum iha arhasi)

- कर्म कर्तुम् Karma kartum – To act, to perform prescribed action.
- इह Iha – Here, in this life, in this world of duties and dharma.
- अर्हसि Arhasi – You ought, you are worthy, you are called to do this.

This final phrase of the final verse of chapter-sixteen is a divine exhortation: having understood the śāstric path, one must act accordingly—not in indifference or impulse, but in full awareness of the soul's journey toward मोक्ष mokṣa through Sanātana-Dharma.

—: In Brief :—

— ॐ श्रीकृष्णाय नमः ॐ —

In contrast to the souls of demoniac nature—who neither know what ought to be done nor what ought to be refrained from (see verse 16.7)—the ones possessed of divine nature are urged to align their life with the śāstric ordinances.

To Arjuna, who initially feared that the battle before him would incur sin, Shri Krishna gently reminds that the fulfillment of one's svadharma—when guided by scriptural wisdom—does not lead to bondage, but rather becomes a sanctified offering on the altar of Sanātana-Dharma.

As was taught earlier (in Gītā 2.32), for the kṣatriya, to rise to battle in a righteous war is an open gate to heaven; and similarly, for all beings, actions rooted in scriptural commandments only purify, and they never defile, whatever be the nature of the work involved.

— ॐ श्रीरामाय नमः ॐ —

The verse also carries a profound philosophical insight: it is not merely outward action, but the inner attitude of dispassion and selflessness, sanctioned by śāstra, that leads to mokśa: God-realization. Remember:

- Action tainted by selfish desire and pride binds;
- Action performed arbitrarily, against the ordinance of śāstra, leads to ruin;
- Action performed in a spirit of surrender, harmonized with the scriptural path, sanctifies human life and leads the soul toward perfection.

What impels Action is knowledge—which comes from śāstras.

— ॐ रामेश्वराय नमः ॐ —

The Lord has concluded this chapter by bestowing all seekers with an infallible guide: the शास्त्र śāstras—the authentic scriptures of Sanātana-Dharma.

The śāstras alone are capable of illumining our path, distinguishing what elevates from what degrades, what purifies from what defiles.

Knowing this, all of us are enjoined to live not by caprice, but by the wisdom of the ages—performing only those acts endorsed by the śāstras, and abstaining from what they forbid.

— ॐ धर्मरक्षकाय नमः ॐ —

Most importantly, to perform the prescribed acts free of attachments is paramount—driven by a spirit which stays rooted in service to Krishna and His Sanātana-Dharma—for only such actions open the gateway to liberation.

With this, the Lord has prepared the groundwork for the teachings to follow next —the final two chapters where He will further unveil the mysteries of karma, jnāna, tyaga and bhakti that lead to union with the Divine.

The Bhagavad-Gitā scripture is a lamp unshaken by the wind; it measures us, spells out our duty, reveals the way. To walk by its light is to step steady, sure, toward the highest pinnacle—where we one day realize: who I am.

Come O mortal, let us tread the path of Gītā-Dharma—the entirety of Sanātana-Dharma encapsulated in a mere 700 verses of the Bhagavad-Gītā. It is the most beautiful beatifying thing on earth.

— ॐ तत सत ॐ —

Before we move on, let us bow in reverence to this sacred verse. Write it by hand, reflect on its meaning, chant it aloud, make it your own.

— ॐ —

तस्माच्छास्त्रं प्रमाणं ते कार्याकार्यव्यवस्थितौ ।
tasmācchāstraṁ pramāṇaṁ te kāryākāryavyavasthitau
ज्ञात्वा शास्त्रविधानोक्तं कर्म कर्तुमिहार्हसि ॥ १६-२४ ॥
jñātvā śāstravidhānoktaṁ karma kartumihārhasi (16-24)

—ॐ—
तस्माच्छास्त्रं प्रमाणं ते कार्याकार्यव्यवस्थितौ ।
tasmācchāstraṁ pramāṇaṁ te kāryākāryavyavasthitau
ज्ञात्वा शास्त्रविधानोक्तं कर्म कर्तुमिहार्हसि ॥ १६-२४ ॥
jñātvā śāstravidhānoktaṁ karma kartumihārhasi (16-24)

ॐ तत्सदिति श्रीमद्भगवद्गीतासूपनिषत्सु ब्रह्मविद्यायां योगशास्त्रे श्रीकृष्णार्जुनसंवादे
om tatsaditi śrīmadbhagavadgītāsūpaniṣatsu brahmavidyāyāṁ yogaśāstre śrīkṛṣṇārjunasaṁvāde
दैवासुरसम्पद्विभागयोगो नाम षोडशोऽध्यायः श्लोकः २४
daivāsurasampadvibhāgayogo nāma ṣoḍaśo'dhyāyaḥ ślokaḥ 24

Om-Tat-Sat—Om (Braham) is the sole Reality. In the Yogic Scripture on the Science-of-Braham, the Shrimada-Bhāgvada-Gītā Upanishad, we hereby conclude Shloka 24 of the Dialogue between Shrī Krishna and Arjuna entitled Daivāsura-Sampada-Vibhāga-Yoga, Canto XVI.

A Soul Adrift Without the Guide of Shastras शास्त्र

O me, how often have I walked by Whim, not by the Word,
Desiring freedom, I cast aside the Wisdom—which as child I had heard.
I chose what pleased the moment in time,
and spurned what tried my patience and pride,
But every path I carved, driven by convenience's whim,
soon became a wasteland inside.

O fool, thou hadst the Gita in thy hand—
a map to the Ātmā—to heights sublime,
Yet thou chased just flesh and dreams —
heeding not Krishna's Voice-Divine!

O Mortal: Without the beacon of Shastra's Light—
-By which the ancients steered through the Night,
-By which Dharma, humanity through the ages, managed to survive,
—How else couldst thou know what ought be done, and what to avoid?

Now an Ignoramus—unmoored from Shastras—my soul drifts.
Drifts where?—To where the loudest voices cry, sing.
I converge to gurus who merchandize well—
Who have the largest followers & likes.

Charming hawks sell what the flock likes to hear:
Sweet Lies in polished phrase.
Not Truth, but Ease is peddled now—in borrowed Vedic haze.
Their gospel? Comfort, screens, ease—No thorns of penance, No 3-strikes.

They vend a god who demands no tyaga, no penance,
no effort, no vow, no silence—rather who pampers with Indulgence.
Welcome to the new faith of the new-age—slick and packaged well.
No exertion, no travail—and stripped from the brow all sweat.

Neo-gurus have cast aside the Gita-Dharma—the true scriptural flame,
And carved out new laws, new brands—in their own names.
No tapas burns within their eyes, No silence greets their inner skies.

And rightly so—for today's Seeker burns not for Truth—
He just needs enough to fool himself—and to bow to EASY's call.
Silver-tongued men, in well-dressed robes serve so well his purpose.
What enthralls the flock is: pomp, show, songs; miracles, mystery, tales;
It's perfect match made in Heaven—they deserve each other so well.

Cheats take the husk of sacred writ—wrap it around their lies,
A new-made creed of softness spun—with ancient fire snuffed out.

Their words are slick, Ashramas more sleek—teachings new & bold,
Hollowed minds & hearts, brought into camps—herded, milched, sold.

Staying in luxuries, they know not Penance—or Tyaga's burning fire.
Charlatan, frauds, mimics they are—trying to echo the Rishis' lyre.

So be Warned O man: What's being sold to thee is likely NOT Shastra शास्त्र.

ॐ Chapter-Sixteen Recap

— ॐ तत सत ॐ —

As we take leave of the sixteenth-canto of the Bhagavad-Gītā, "Daivāsura-Sampad-Vibhāga Yoga", we do not depart lightly.

This chapter did not merely instruct—it revealed, with crystalline clarity, the inner architecture of human nature, showing us the dual tendencies embedded within the fabric of existence: the divine (daivī) and the demoniac (āsurī).

It invited us not only to understand but to discern—to purify, to choose, and to align one's life with the luminous path of Ekam-Sanātana-Dharma—the true religion, the one and only.

— ॐ —

We were shown that true spirituality is not confined to outward form or fleeting emotion—it is a matter of inner disposition, of the qualities cultivated, cherished, and lived. In this chapter, the Lord did not offer abstract speculation but instead held up a mirror, allowing us to look deeply into our own nature and to examine the subtle impulses that shape our destinies.

In broad strokes:

We learnt that the divine qualities—humility, truthfulness, non-injury, self-restraint, compassion, and reverence for the Divine—lead the soul toward liberation.

By contrast, the demoniac traits—arrogance, hypocrisy, harshness, delusion, and heedlessness—draw the soul downward into bondages, sufferings, and darkness.

We discovered that this inner constitution, more than circumstance or ritual, governs the soul's journey.

Now let us gently retrace the sacred contours of this chapter, in the order of themes revealed therein:

— o —

At the outset, through **verses 1 to 3**, we were graced with a luminous enumeration of the divine virtues. These qualities, born of sattva and ripened through spiritual discipline, are the ornaments of the seeker who walks the path of righteousness. They form the moral and spiritual foundation of one destined for liberation.

— o —

Thereafter, in **verses 4 to 5**, the demoniac tendencies were outlined—of those born predominantly with tamas and rajas gunas -

marked by cruelty, deceit, and a lack of inner purity. We were reminded that these do not merely taint conduct, but shape one's very being, determining whether one ascends or falls in the cosmic journey.

—o—

In **verses 6 through 8**, we examined the contrasting worldviews of the divine and the demoniac. The former recognize order, law, and the Supreme as the substratum of all; the latter deny such foundations, imagining a universe born of lust, without purpose or inner law. This deviation from truth is not merely intellectual—it leads to unrighteous conduct and inner ruin.

—o—

Verses 9 to 12 described the life-patterns of the āsuric soul—driven by insatiable desire, entangled in anxiety, ambition, and pride, endlessly multiplying actions without meaning or sanctity. This life, though adorned outwardly with power and possession, is barren of peace.

—o—

In **verses 13 to 17**, we observed the boastful inner speech of the demoniac—their belief in their own autonomy, their mockery of dharma, and their intoxication with ego and achievement. Blind to impermanence and the higher law, they fall deeper into ignorance.

—o—

Then, in **verses 18 to 20**, we saw the karmic consequence of such a life: rebirth in lower realms, severance from the Divine, and entrapment in ever-darkening cycles. The Lord's words here were not wrathful, but solemn—expressing the gravity of moral causality.

—o—

Yet, a door to freedom was opened in **verses 21 to 22**, where we were warned of the threefold gateway to hell—lust, anger, and greed. By abandoning these, the soul begins to ascend. Those who reject this triple-doom and live by higher discernment, walk the path of purity and attain to the Supreme.

—o—

Finally, in **verses 23 and 24**, the Lord affirmed the centrality of śāstra—the sacred revelation—as the guiding light in determining what is to be done and what is to be renounced. One who acts capriciously, ignoring divine counsel, falls from grace; but one who lives in accordance with śāstra walks in harmony with the cosmic order.

—ॐ—

Thus, in this canto, we learned not merely what to renounce or perform, but how to perceive rightly, how to read the script of our own hearts, and how to align with the divine order that upholds all creation.

This teaching was not harsh, but precise; not condemning, but clarifying. It called us to vigilance—not fear—but a noble attentiveness to the sacred within.

The battle between divine and demoniac is not outside us, but within. And the choice to nourish one or the other is the choice between bondage and liberation, between sorrow and enduring joy.

So let us take this wisdom into our heart and cultivate the divine qualities with steadfast strength, casting away the shadows of ignorance, and offering our lives—moment by moment, day by blessed day —at the altar of the Eternal. For this, indeed, is the way of Gītā-Dharma: not to command from above, but to awaken from within.

ॐ तत्सदिति श्रीमद्भगवद्गीतासूपनिषत्सु ब्रह्मविद्यायां योगशास्त्रे श्रीकृष्णार्जुनसंवादे
om tatsaditi śrīmadbhagavadgītāsūpaniṣatsu brahmavidyāyāṁ yogaśāstre śrīkṛṣṇārjunasaṁvāde
दैवासुरसम्पद्विभागयोगो नाम षोडशोऽध्यायः ॥
daivāsurasampadvibhāgayogo nāma ṣoḍaśo'dhyāyaḥ .

Om-Tat-Sat—Om (Braham) is the sole Reality. In this Yogic Scripture on the Science of Brahama—the Shrimada-Bhāgvada-Gītā Upanishad—hereby ends the dialogue between Shrī Krishna and Arjuna entitled: Daivāsura-Sampada-Vibhāga Yoga, Canto XVI

—o—

[O Seeker, we thank thee for reading thus far. This has been a brief commentary and lots still remains unsaid. Rāma-willing, our exhaustive commentary will become available starting 2027. This is our init endeavor and surely it's full of many faults which we fully own—and we pray you will take it in thy heart to pardon us. We have endeavored to keep our commentary opinion-free. The poesy "fillers"—which utilize the blank spaces at end of chapters—might be construed to be opinionated though. Bhagavad-Gita is a celestial stream and any human touch, however well-meaning, only sullies it some. We hope to be forgiven by Bhagwana Shri Krishna for daring to torture this sublime text of His, which has no parallels anywhere—never will.]

ॐ ॐ ॐ ॐ ॐ ॐ ॐ ॐ ॐ ॐ ॐ ॐ ॐ ॐ ॐ ॐ ॐ ॐ

ॐ गीतामाहात्म्यम् GĪTĀ-MĀHĀTMYAM

[Verses on the glory and import of the Bhagavad-Gītā]

— ॐ —

गीताशास्त्रमिदं पुण्यं यः पठेत्प्रयतः पुमान् ।
gītāśāstramidaṁ puṇyaṁ yaḥ paṭhetprayataḥ pumān ,
विष्णोः पदमवाप्नोति भयशोकादिवर्जितः ॥
viṣṇoḥ padamavāpnoti bhayaśokādivarjitaḥ .

One who diligently studies this Bhagavad-Gītā—the bestower of all virtues—with firm devotion and a regulated mind—verily attains Vaikuntha—the holy abode of Māhā-Vishnu—and he stands freed of all the fears and sorrows of this mundane world.

— ॐ —

गीताध्ययनशीलस्य प्राणायामपरस्य च ।
gītādhyayanaśīlasya prāṇāyāmaparasya ca ,
नैव सन्ति हि पापानि पूर्वजन्मकृतानि च ॥
naiva santi hi pāpāni pūrvajanmakṛtāni ca .

One who performs Prāṇāyāms and studies the Bhagavad-Gītā regularly and sincerely—all his sins melt away, even those from all prior lives.

— ॐ —

मलनिर्मोचनं पुंसां जलस्नानं दिने दिने ।
malanirmocanaṁ puṁsāṁ jalasnānaṁ dine dine ,
सकृद्गीताम्भसि स्नानं संसारमलनाशनम् ॥
sakṛdgītāmbhasi snānaṁ saṁsāramalanāśanam .

A daily bath removes external bodily taints, but a single bath in the sacred waters of Bhagavad-Gītā is enough to remove all the taints of this Saṁsāra—this polluting worldly existence of joys, sorrows, births, and deaths.

— ॐ —

गीता सुगीता कर्तव्या किमन्यैः शास्त्रविस्तरैः ।
gītā sugītā kartavyā kimanyaiḥ śāstravistaraiḥ ,
या स्वयं पद्मनाभस्य मुखपद्माद्विनिःसृता ॥
yā svayaṁ padmanābhasya mukhapadmādviniḥsṛtā .

Why go in for other elaborate scriptures, when you can chant the Gītā—the essence of all Vedic scriptures—which issued forth from the lotus mouth of Māhā-Vishnu Himself—on whose navel is the lotus of Creation.

— ॐ —

भारतामृतसर्वस्वं विष्णोर्वक्त्राद्विनिःसृतम् ।
bhāratāmṛtasarvasvaṁ viṣṇorvaktrādviniḥsṛtam ,
गीतागङ्गोदकं पीत्वा पुनर्जन्म न विद्यते ॥
gītāgaṅgodakaṁ pītvā punarjanma na vidyate .

There is no more rebirth for one who partakes of the sacred waters of the Gītā-Gangā—the holy stream which flowed out from the lotus lips of Shri Māhā-Vishnu—the nectar which is the quintessence of Māhā-Bhārata.

— ॐ —

एकं शास्त्रं देवकीपुत्रगीतमेको देवो देवकीपुत्र एव ।
ekaṁ śāstraṁ devakīputragītameko devo devakīputra eva ,
एको मन्त्रस्तस्य नामानि यानि कर्माप्येकं तस्य देवस्य सेवा ॥
eko mantrastasya nāmāni yāni karmāpyekaṁ tasya devasya sevā .

The holy Gītā of Krishna—son of Devakī—is the One Scripture; Krishna—son of Devakī—is the One God; the name Krishna—son of Devakī—is the One Mantra; service to Him—son of Devakī—is the One and only Duty.

— ॐ —

श्रीकृष्णचरणार्पणमस्तु
śrī kṛṣṇa caraṇāarpaṇamastu
(Hereby dedicated to the Lotus Feet of Bhagwāna Shri Krishna)

कायेन वाचा मनसेंद्रियैर्वा । बुद्ध्यात्मना वा प्रकृतिस्वभावात् ।
kāyena vācā manaseṁdriyairvā , buddhyātmanā vā prakritisvabhāvāt ,
करोमि यद्यत् सकलं परस्मै । नारायणायेति समर्पयामि ॥
karomi yadyat sakalaṁ parasmai , nārāyaṇāyeti samarpayāmi .

Whatever it is I do—through body, mind, speech, or sense-organs, or with my intellect and soul, or with my innate natural tendencies—whatever it be—I offer it all unto Narayana (Bhagwāna Shri Krishna / Bhagwāna Shri Rāma).

Ekam-Sanātana-Dharma
एकं सनातन धर्म
Only-True-Religion

— ॐ —

या गीता सनातनस्य धर्मस्यामृतरूपिणी । लोकानां मार्गदर्शिनी तस्याः मूलं प्रयच्छामि ॥
yā gītā sanātanasya dharmasyāmṛtarūpiṇī , lokānāṁ margadarśinī tasyāḥ mūlaṁ prayacchāmi .

That Gītā, which's the nectar-form of Sanātana Dharma—the guide of the worlds upon The-Path—towards Her sacred roots I now proceed to take refuge.

स्वयं प्रेरितो प्रेरय मित्रबान्धवम् । गीता-ज्ञानस्य दीपं सर्वहृदि दीपय ॥
svayaṃ prērito prēraya mitra-bāndhavam , gītā-jñānasya dīpaṃ sarva-hṛdi dīpaya .

Be inspired and inspire thy friends and companions. Light the Lamp of Gītā-Wisdom in all hearts.

Be Inspired and Inspire Others. Light a Lamp of Wisdom.
Start your own Gitā Classes with a Friend Today.

www.ingramcontent.com/pod-product-compliance
Lightning Source LLC
Chambersburg PA
CBHW081430070526
44586CB00020B/2540
* 9 7 8 1 9 4 5 7 3 9 7 6 7 *